From the

Agility Foundation Training for Puppies and Beginner Dogs

Kim Collins

This book is dedicated to my mom.
Without her, none of this would
be possible.

And to Piper, a dream dog, who introduced me
to the sport of agility and made everything so easy.
Little did I know what I was getting into!
Thank you for being so amazing
and for leading me gently and honestly into the
wonderful world of dogs.

Ruzam's Misty Piper
Winner 2000 USDAA Grand Prix 16" class
Del Mar, California
Winner 2001 AAC Nationals 10" Specials Class
Calgary, Alta
Winner 2004 AAC Nationals 6" Vets Class
Montreal, Quebec
First Mini dog to earn the AAC ATChC title

From the Ground Up: Agility Foundation Training for Puppies and Beginner Dogs

Dogwise Publishing
403 South Mission Street
Wenatchee, Washington 98801
800-776-2665
www.dogwise.com

Design: Katharine Webb
Editor: Anne Douglas
Photography by Kim Collins, Rob Collins, Pam Earl, Photoplay's Portrait, Sheldon Pineo, Len Silvester, Rob Struthers, Dixon Zalit
Cover photo: Steve Surfman Photography

From the Ground Up

Agility Foundation Training for
Puppies and Beginner Dogs

By Kim Collins

Photograph by Dixon Zalit

Contents

Acknowledgements

When I first started training agility in 1996, I had no idea what was involved in this sport. I had been competing in obedience for about three years with my two Shelties when my good friend, June Barton, talked me into coming with her to an agility lesson. I was hooked. A group of us started a club and I was voted the first agility director because I had taken that one agility lesson, which was one more than everyone else had taken!

There were no other agility clubs or trainers in our immediate area, so we were on our own. I collected as much information from books, videos, and the Internet as I could. During my search for information, I met Kay Whitehead, who lived about an hour away.

Kay had a lovely Border Collie named Flare who was an amazing obedience and agility dog. She was also completely deaf. Watching Kay work with Flare made me realize that dogs are magnificent creatures with hearts of gold. Flare never had a correction administered to her… ever. Kay felt that just the fact that this dog was trying to learn these sports was incredible. Flare learned solely through positive reinforcement. I learned an incredible amount about how dogs think and learn from Kay and Flare and I quickly realized that there was a whole lot more to training agility – and dogs in general – than I first thought.

In 1999, our club hosted a seminar with Susan Garrett. Susan introduced us to the concept of clicker training and the use of toys as well as food as a reinforcer. It was then that everything fell into place for me. This was probably one of the most enlightening and humbling times of my dog training career. Susan made me realize how important building a relationship with my dog is, how everything in life needs to be fun for them, how to use toys and games to increase their enthusiasm for learning, and how important it is that I become a better trainer before I expect my dogs to get better. I continue to attend Say Yes camps and work with Susan and the Say Yes instructors as often as I can.

Since 1999, I have had the opportunity to work with many other fabulous trainers and handlers. This has allowed me to pick up many great teaching, handling and training ideas over the years. Thank you to Kathy

Keats, Nancy Ouellette, Theresa Rector, Wendy Pape, Jen Pinder, Stacey Peardot-Goudy, Stuart and Pati Mah and Linda Mecklenberg. Much of the information in this book is a collection of their ideas that I have adapted to fit into my own training program.

Trimine's Solar Flare

The program we use at Pawsitive Steps has not been developed through my efforts alone. My instructors have been amazing in their continued support of everything I have done. They have covered for me and held down the fort when I have been away so much. They are always open to trying new things and they keep me on my toes with all their questions. Thank you to Donna, Michelle, Michelle, Shannon, and Brenda. You are an amazing group of trainers!

Also, I must thank my other half, Rob Struthers, who puts up with all of us girls at the centre and keeps me from going to the dogs; seven is quite enough, I know! Without you, I would not be doing any of this.

I also need to give a special thank you to my mom, Pat. She was the one who started and fostered my love of dogs and dog training from the time I was born. I have always had a dog in my home and some form of dog training in my life. Without her, I would not be doing what I am doing and loving it so much.

I need to thank all my students, from those here in Prince George who train at Pawsitive Steps, to the outreach groups in Nova Scotia, BC and Alberta, and the repeat students I see at my seminars. I am always amazed at how committed they are and how impressive their dogs are. I enjoy every minute I get to work with them.

I am so grateful to all the dogs in my life, past and present. Ceildhe, Piper, Bryn, Feyd, Sierra, Warder, Peak and Bounce. They are wonderfully honest and enthusiastic and all so very different to live with and train. They have taught me so much about their species. I treasure every minute I get with them. I know that I still have a lot to learn, and I owe it to all my dogs to learn as much as possible to improve our communication and make learning even more fun.

Thank you to the following dog "models": Cai, Chime, Colleen, Bryn, Tristan, Bounce, Peak, Toque, Rayn, Sierra, Kess, Kate, Mitch, and Pepper.

About the Author

Kim Collins has lived with dogs all her life and has been training dogs professionally since 1992. After starting with competitive obedience, Kim quickly discovered the growing sport of agility in 1995. Kim went on to win the 2000 USDAA National Agility Championship with her Shetland Sheepdog, Piper, and three Canadian National Agility Championships, two with Piper and one with her Border Collie, Feyd. Kim has also won seven Regional Agility Championships with three different dogs. Kim and her two Border Collies, Bryn and Feyd, were members of the Agility Association of Canada's 2004 IFCS Canadian World Team and traveled to Valencia, Spain to compete.

Back row: Feyd, Bounce, Bryn and Peak. Front row: Warder, Piper and Sierra.

Kim trials in a variety of venues. She competes in obedience with the Canadian Kennel Club (CKC) and the Canadian Association of Rally Obedience (CARO). In agility, she trials in a variety of organizations, including the Agility Association of Canada (AAC), the United States Dog Agility Association (USDAA), and the North American Dog Agility Council (NADAC).

Kim owns and operates Pawsitive Steps Canine Sports Centre in Prince George, British Columbia, Canada. Pawsitive Steps is a large indoor, year-round training facility dedicated solely to the promotion of positive, non-aggressive training techniques for pet and performance dogs. Kim teaches seminars all over Canada and started an outreach program in 2002 dedicated to helping handlers in other cities who want to train using positive techniques. She currently has students all over western Canada as well as over 200 students in her own facility in Prince George. She is an AAC Masters level Agility judge, is a member of the Canadian Association of Professional Pet Dog Trainers and was a workshop presenter at their 2003 Conference.

Kim and Piper winning the USDAA Grand Prix

Kim's teaching background comes from spending 20 years as a dance teacher and choreographer teaching all levels and ages of students. She now devotes herself full time to helping people and their dogs develop positive relationships through education, training and canine sports. All of Kim's training methods — with people and dogs — are motivational and positive. Visit her web site at www.pawsitivesteps.ca.

The Sport of Agility

Agility is truly one of the most fun things you can do with your dog. The sport has grown so fast in the last 20 years that it is hard to keep up. There are a variety of organizations sanctioning the sport and two different world championships, both held overseas, as well as many great national championship events in North America. Getting started in the sport just takes a click on the computer to introduce you to a whole world of agility enthusiasts out there. Most of these people are more than happy to help someone new get started.

In North America, we have many great organizations, all promoting agility, all with a different outlook on the sport. There is the United States Dog Agility Association (USDAA) based in Texas; the North American

Photograph by Dixon Zalit

Dog Agility Council (NADAC) based in Idaho; the Australian Shepherd Club of America (ASCA) which runs under NADAC rules; the American (AKC) and Canadian (CKC) Kennel Clubs that have agility programs and sponsor our World Teams; the United Kennel Club (UKC), the Agility Association of Canada (AAC), and Canine Performance Events (CPE). All of these organizations have various memberships, newsletters, magazines, and web sites for more information on getting involved in the sport of agility. Their contact information is listed at the back of this book.

One of the most wonderful things about this sport is that any dog — mixed breed or purebred — may compete as long as he is physically and mentally sound. There is no restriction on the handler's soundness, though! Anyone, young or old, small or large, can compete in this sport and have a fabulous time doing it. The people you meet in agility are absolutely the best. Everyone has such a wonderful attitude about their dogs and most are out at the trials to visit with friends, old and new, and just plain have fun! Not only do the handlers love it, but the dogs love it too.

So if you are picking up this book as a "new to agility" person, welcome to the sport! I hope you have as much fun doing it as I have. If you are reading this book as an experienced agility competitor and are looking for tips for your next agility dog I hope you get some helpful ideas.

Before You Get Started

Before you start training for agility there are a few things that you might want to consider to make sure this sport is fun and safe for both you and your pooch. I see many people doing this sport who, in my opinion, do not develop a strong enough relationship with their dogs before they start training. This sport requires the dog to try many things that, initially, he may not be comfortable with. It is imperative that the dog completely trusts the handler and that the handler has a relationship with the dog that will never jeopardize that trust.

The Relationship with Your Dog

It really doesn't matter how good a handler or trainer you are, your dog is yours for life. He must first be your dog — your pet, your buddy, and your best friend. You can always improve your handling and your training abilities, but it is your relationship with your dog that must always come first. This is only a game we play with our dogs. It is not life and death — you must work together, trust each other and respect each other as living, breathing beings. Try to keep this in mind when you hit rough spots in your training sessions. And you will hit those spots — we all do. But they are not insurmountable and it really isn't worth getting upset with your dog over a glitch in your training session.

Another consideration is the dog's mental state. Some dogs, especially males, mature very late. Older or rescue dogs may have some confidence issues they may need to overcome before they begin

Your relationship with your dog should come first.

a training program. Be careful not to push these dogs to do things that will make them more fearful and mistrust you. Take time to build the trust into your relationship with your dog. I have had to do different things at different times with each of my dogs based on personality. And just because a dog is bossy and pushy at home doesn't mean he will be that way in training (I wish!).

Learn to read your dog. What the dog shows you when he is learning is honest. Don't assume that the dog is feeling something other than what he is showing you. Look at the behaviour of the dog and make changes based on what you see at that very moment. Your dog will never lie to you.

Health and Fitness

Agility is a very physical activity and there is always a risk of injury to your dog if you are not careful about his health and fitness. You should always make sure that your dog is physically and mentally capable of doing the work before you start any kind of training that requires jumping, twisting, turning or climbing. It's a good idea to get a physical exam and a set of X-rays done by a qualified veterinarian to ensure there are no structural problems with the shoulders or hips.

If the dog is young, be very careful not to train anything that requires any jumping or weaving until the growth plates have closed. X-rays can verify whether they have. Some dogs can take a long time to mature physically. It is not breed- or litter-specific; dogs within the same litter can have growth plates close at completely different times. I recommend checking each dog individually by X-rays.

With an older or rescue dog, you should have X-rays done of the hips, elbows and shoulders to ensure the dog is sound. Eye problems are common and should also be watched for. We really want to make sure that the dogs are not being asked to do something that is painful due to a physical problem. This takes the enjoyment out of the sport for the dog and can often lead to mental and physical "shut down."

The weight of the dog is also of extreme importance and the most common problem we see in the adult dogs that come for classes. Most dogs that are considered a healthy weight for a pet dog are too heavy for this sport. Your dog will need to be on the slim side of healthy for their breed. Puppies also need to be kept healthy but light as they grow to avoid damage to their joints. You should be able to feel the dog's ribs and hip bones with the flat of your hand. If you can't, the dog likely needs to lose a bit of weight.

Most dogs that are considered a healthy weight for a pet are too heavy for agility.

Personality and Breed Traits

Every dog is different. Dogs of the same age and breed or even from the same litter can have very different temperaments, working styles, and structure. Try to take all this into consideration when you start your dog in agility.

When I got my Sheltie, Peak, I knew right from the beginning that she was not going to be a dog that would just jump in with all four feet like the Border Collies even though at home she was always the first one out the door for the toy. She needed to be introduced to things at her own speed, in her own time. I also knew I had to introduce her to things like a tippy board, dogwalk plank, jump standards, and chute fabric long before I actually tried to train anything formally. I used my clicker to let her experiment with these things by letting her touch them, step on them, go around them and anything else she wanted to do. That way, when it came time to train the equipment associated with these things, she had already seen parts of them and they were not as intimidating to her.

My Border Collies all have different personalities as well. Bryn, my first

Every dog is different... especially dogs of different breeds.

Border Collie, is very careful, and can easily be intimidated socially by other dogs in crates or ex-pens. She does not like to be pushed or pulled around in any way. I learned a hard lesson from her about trusting your instincts and maintaining your relationship with your dog when I attended a seminar and the instructor wanted us to put our dogs on leash to get them to come down the contact on the A-frame faster. Against my better judgment I did it, not wanting to offend the instructor or seem like a "know-it-all." Bryn, however, was not happy about this procedure. She did come down faster (she had no choice as we were pulling her down with the leash!). But when they told me to try it without the leash, she left the ring as soon as the leash came off and didn't want to go near the A-frame again. I was very angry with myself for allowing this to happen in the first place. I should have trusted my instincts.

My other two Border Collies are pretty "easy keepers" and will try anything. I trained them in a very hands-off style; they were never pushed or pulled into or onto anything. They were always allowed to bail off equipment if they chose to. I will never force a dog to do something. If I think the dog is mentally capable of working through the issue I will try to help him work through it. If I think the dog is too stressed, we back off and try another route — which usually consists of breaking the behaviour down to smaller steps using a clicker. It also helps to work with a very hungry or energetic dog!

Try to experiment with things like sound, motion, height, and texture underfoot with your dog at home and see what kinds of things he is nervous about. Does he not like to walk on linoleum? How about slats like you have on a sundeck? What about open-backed stairs? Will he burrow under a blanket or does he get freaked when his head is covered up? Will he jump on the bed or couch? Will he walk along a log when you take him out for a walk? Does he choose to jump over things in his way or go under or around them? Is he easily startled by metal dog dishes being dropped on the floor? How about keys being dropped? These are all things that will tell you something about your dog and the approach you will want to take when you start your training.

Commitment

If you decide to get involved with this sport, make sure that you truly love to train. The time you will spend training far, far exceeds the time you will spend competing and collecting ribbons and qualifying rounds! If you enjoy training and spending time teaching your dog and yourself new things you will have a long and wonderful career in this sport! And I will be honest with you: agility is addictive, and agility training, whether you want to train recreationally or compete at national level, is time and cost intensive. You may go in saying, "I just want to do something fun with my dog" and then, wham! You are addicted.

Many agility addicts have sold their homes to buy land for the dogs and all the equipment, or have sold their cars to get a vehicle that will fit all the dogs in crates and pull a travel trailer. Some have quit their high (ok, not so high) paying jobs to train and teach full time. There should be a warning on the registration form for classes just like they have on cigarette packages:

WARNING: Agility can be hazardous to your bank account.

I was one of those people who started out just wanting to be a better trainer and handler for my dogs, as I felt they deserved that. I wanted to learn to run the smoothest course I could. In my quest for that, I was lucky enough to learn some really fascinating things about training and handling dogs, and that has been the most rewarding experience of my career. As I became a better handler and trainer, the titles and awards just kind of happened. Winning a national championship was never a goal of mine — it became a side effect of better training and handling.

So don't underestimate yourself or your dog! Just the fact that you have picked up this book means you are interested in learning about the sport. Remember, 80 per cent of success is showing up! Read on to find out more of what I have learned in my agility career that has helped me and my dogs become a better team. I hope some of what I have learned will help you and your dogs enjoy the sport as much as we do.

Training Basics

When I started training my dogs for agility it seemed that I always had more to learn than my dog. And it seemed that my dog could do things for other trainers that I couldn't get her to do myself. This was frustrating at times, and I really had to face up to the "it's not the dog's fault" theory. That phrase will follow you wherever you go. And it is 100 per cent true! I had lots to learn about handling, footwork, timing, cue systems, distance training, jump training and the fact that my mechanical skills were not always great.

When we watch agility competitions, many handlers make it look so easy that we think we should just be able to teach our dog to do the equipment and then presto, they can run a course! I have learned over the years that there is a bit more to it than that. There are many different parts to the sport, and each part needs to be trained separately and with patience. Going too fast can be extremely detrimental to your dog and your relationship on course. This was my first big lesson and the most important one I can pass along. Take your time! Enjoy the learning and training process as you will spend many more hours and much more money on your training than you ever will on competitions! Competitions are, in my mind, a way to test my training program and find out what we are weak on as a team. As an added bonus, they are great social events where you get to visit with friends from near and far.

One of the first things handlers need to do is to understand how dogs think and learn. There is extensive information out there regarding types of training methods. Choose a method that makes sense to you. Make sure you are happy with the results. The training methods I use can be started on a puppy as young as eight weeks old and used all the way through their adult training. Any method that cannot be used on an eight-week-old puppy is probably not a method I would use to train my dogs. If you hear someone tell you not to start training until the dog is six months to a year old, it is likely that the methods they are using are too harsh.

Be careful of training programs that claim to be fast, or that use no rewards. I saw a sign on a telephone pole the other day that read "Dog Training in your Home — Only One Lesson Needed." With all the scientific data available regarding how animals learn, these are just plain ridiculous promotional tactics. There are no quick fixes or "train your dog in six easy lessons" methods out there that really work. To learn, dogs need time, patience, change of location, reinforcement, opportunity to make choices, and repetition. So an eight-week agility class that has you on all the equipment by the end of eight classes is not teaching you or the dog anything.

The best thing you can do for your dog is to become a better and more skilled trainer. Allow yourself some time to work on your own skills either at a seminar or with another trainer. Developing your mechanical skills is something you need to practice, often without the dog. Try to remember this when you get stuck during training. Is it the dog or do you need to go back and allow yourself time to learn how to do the skill before you try to teach it to your dog?

Our dogs are limited only by their physical capabilities and our ability to train them. Before you start, be very clear in your own mind exactly what you want to train, and how you want to train it. By making your training sessions too difficult, you may actually train problems you hadn't intended to.

Finally, keep in mind that behaviour is always changing; therefore it can always be changed. Never give up on your dog and your training. If you don't like something you have trained, either inadvertently or on purpose, then re-teach it, re-name it, and reward the new behaviour a lot. Not to say that re-teaching is going to be easy... it's not. The first behaviour the dog learns is always strongest, so think about exactly the kind of behaviour you want to train and teach it correctly from the beginning. But you can re-train if you want to. If, at any time in your initial training, you see behaviours crop up that you don't like but aren't sure how to get rid of, stop. Re-evaluate your training session or find someone who can help you fix the problem.

Understanding Dogs

A dog is a product of his environment, genetics, and his trainer's ability to communicate effectively. He learns that his actions have direct and immediate consequences. His learning is affected by his hard-wiring with inherited breed traits. He learns through your interactions with him on a daily basis. Everything you do with your dog is teaching him something. You must decide if your interactions with him are teaching him something you want him to know or not. Often we are teaching our dogs things and we don't even know it!

It always seems to me that my dogs pick up behaviours that I don't want them to know in about 30 seconds and they remember it for a lifetime, and the skills I do want them to know seem to take forever to train!

Here are three key concepts to remember about dogs:

1. Dogs are energy efficient.
This means they will always try to find the shortest, easiest route to what they want. They are genetically predisposed to expend the least amount of energy they have to in order to get what they want or need. This is how they survived in the wild. Therefore, when your dog cuts behind you on a turn instead of coming to the front where you want him, understand that it is a function of genetics — not stubbornness. You have to let him know that the only way to get what he wants is to do it your way, which in his mind may be the long way.

2. Dogs are reinforcement driven.
In other words, they will do what they have to do to get what they want. If they don't want what you have, they will not expend energy trying to get it (read: energy efficient). They are not necessarily disinterested in the whole thing; you just haven't provided them with a reason to work. So it is up to you to make sure you know what your dog wants and how much energy he will choose to use to get it.

3. Dogs will always ask two questions: "Why?" and "Why not?"
Why should I jump over that thing? Why not run off to sniff the fence, chase the squirrel, visit the people, play with that dog? You must be able to answer these questions convincingly for your dog. "Because I say so" is just not a convincing argument. It sounds lame when we say it to children, and even more so when we say it to dogs! Provide your dog with a reason to do what you want. Make it fun and worth his while to participate.

Methods of Training

There are differences between luring, prompting, and shaping a behaviour. We use all three when we train and there are advantages and disadvantages to each.

Luring

Luring is when you use food or a toy (or even a target plate or wires on weave poles) to get the dog to perform a behaviour. We use lures frequently in agility and although luring seems easy to many people, it actually takes quite a bit of knowledge for luring to be effective. It's important to know how to fade your lures as quickly as possible.

Luring is when you use food or a toy or even a target plate to get the dog to perform a behaviour.

Many novice trainers like to lure their dogs as it seems to be the fastest way to get the end behaviour, and it will definitely look like the dog is learning. Unfortunately, it takes many, many repetitions with the lure, and then a systematic fading of the lure, to get the dog to offer the behaviour without the lure.

Most people get stuck on the step of fading the lure. Many dogs have been inadvertently trained not to do anything until they see the lure. Rather than being patient and waiting for the dog to offer something close to the behaviour, people panic and pull out the cookie because they are afraid the dog will lose the behaviour all together if they don't! Pulling out the cookies because your dog won't do something is rewarding him for not doing anything. Be careful your dog is not training you to feed him when he becomes confused. If he is confused and unable to offer the behaviour that you have lured, consider that he probably does not understand what you want and try a different method of training it.

A good rule of thumb when luring is to only use your lure three times and then try to get the behaviour without the lure. One exception to this rule is the weave pole chute method with wires: you will need to do many more than three repetitions before you can remove the wires (see "The Chute" on page 99).

If you can't get the dog to offer an attempt at the behaviour without a cookie present, you need to re-evaluate how you trained the behaviour. Maybe you need to prompt the behaviour a bit or maybe shaping would be a better choice.

Prompting

Prompting is similar to luring in that we use our bodies to encourage the dog to offer the behaviour by moving ourselves around. For example, in our pet program, we teach the dogs to sit using prompting. We start with a cookie in hand (luring) and lift the cookie up from his nose so that the dog follows the cookie into a sit. After three times with the cookie, we eliminate the treat from the hand, but we keep the same hand motion. Using the cookie is luring and the hand motion is prompting the sit.

Prompting is similar to luring in that we use our bodies to encourage the dog to offer the behaviour.

Then we add the verbal command, followed by the prompt of the hand signal. Eventually we fade the hand signal. Occasionally a young dog will become confused and not sit on the verbal. We can then add the prompt of the hand signal to help the dog out. However, this should be done with caution because the dog may ultimately learn to wait for the prompt. We see this with dogs that have learned the weave poles with hand prompts (what we call the "weave pole dance"). They only weave if their handlers are right beside them doing the "dance."

Shaping

Shaping a behaviour takes a bit more time and skill but ultimately dogs learn behaviours more reliably because they have to figure it out on their own. It is like a game of 20 questions. The dog does something and the handler uses some kind of marker (a sound, light or word) to say "yes that is (or close to) what I want!" The dog then learns to offer more behaviours in an attempt to get a reward. Dogs quickly learn that they can speed up the rate of rewards by repeating the last thing they did when they got rewarded. Shaping eliminates the need to first show the dog the reward because the dog has to initiate something to make the reward appear. This method gives you remarkable results in a short period of time but does require some experience with, and knowledge of, operant conditioning. If

With shaping, the dog learns to offer behaviours in an attempt to get a reward.

you want more experience with operant conditioning, find a good clicker seminar or an instructor who trains with a clicker using operant conditioning.

Steps in Training

Here are some basic steps in training a new behaviour. As always, there will be exceptions to the rules but these form a general guideline that may help you avoid skipping important steps.

1. **Shape or prompt the new behaviour**
   If you're luring or prompting a simple behaviour, it may happen very quickly, as in a sit or down. If it's a complicated behaviour such as performing an obstacle, or if you're shaping it, you may have to make your initial goal some approximation of the end behaviour, for instance, approaching the obstacle.

2. **Bridge the behaviour**
   This is the connection to the dog's reward or reinforcer. Often it's a click or the word, "Yes!"

3. **Reward the dog with a primary reinforcer**
   The primary reinforcer is usually food or a toy, and it must be something the dog wants. If it is not something the dog wants, and you try to force the dog to take it, it can actually become a punisher. Choose the reinforcer that is appropriate for the behaviour, such as food for stationary behaviours, like sit-stay, and toys for behaviours that the dog needs motion and drive for, like sending to a piece of equipment.

4. **Release**
   From your final behaviour, use whatever word you like (such as "okay!" or "free" or "break") to release the dog from the behaviour before you try it again. Always use a release word after stationary behaviours. The dog must understand when he is allowed to move out of a stationary position.

5. **Play and praise**
   Take some time to play with your dog and tell him how wonderful he is between each session. If you are using food, only use five to 10 pieces of food and when that is gone, rest the dog. If you're

using a toy as a reinforcer, rest and praise your dog after two minutes of training. In dog training, less is more! If you drill your dog for longer than two or three minutes he will actually stop learning.

6. Reward for speed

Once the dog is happily offering the new behaviour, bit by bit start to raise your criteria for speed. Click only the fast pounce down or the quicker look back at you when you stop moving or the faster sit or the more forceful nose touch. The dog needs to learn to discriminate between the mediocre behaviours and the really great behaviours. This is the stage where you will develop drive and intensity for each behaviour. Do not progress from this stage until you have the drive and intensity you like.

7. Add the command

Once the dog is doing the exercise exactly the way you want to see it done forever — meaning that it's perfectly accurate and fast — add the command. Give the command word as the dog is doing the behaviour, or slightly before he offers it. Don't be in a hurry to name a behaviour unless it is a default behaviour (the one your dog offers first and most often). Name that one quickly and don't reward the dog for that behaviour unless you specifically ask for it.

Don't name partially trained equipment. For example, when training the teeter totter, never name it if the dog is even remotely worried about it. We never want to name a behaviour we don't want to see in the end, such as hesitation on the board. Another example is weave poles. Until the dog is weaving a straight line fast and accurately, don't name them!

8. Initiate a variable rate of reinforcement

Once he is reliably performing the behaviour on a verbal command, start to use a variable rate of reinforcement. Make your rewards random and try to reward the better responses. However, don't get too picky about speed or intensity yet. At this stage we want the dog to learn that he may not get rewarded every time but to keep working because another reward is just around the corner. Do not use variable reinforcement when you're shaping a new behaviour. Keep your rate of reinforcement high and consistent until the behaviour is fully developed.

9. Challenge the dog

Once you are getting a reliable response and can vary your reinforcement, start to challenge the dog's understanding of the exercise. Add distractions that may cause the dog to make an error such as a strategically placed toy or food bag. Work through it. Take it on the road and try it in different locations. You need to know that your dog understands the job no matter where you are or what is around.

10. Take it on the road

Move the behaviour to other locations. You may need to lower the criteria slightly when you change locations. You may even have to start at step one again and re-teach the behaviour in the new location. Work in many locations, keeping the criteria realistic and the distractions limited. Initially, keep the rate of reinforcement very high in each new location. If the rate of reinforcement drops due to the dog being too distracted, find a different location that is not so distracting or lower the criteria.

11. Maintain the behaviour

When he is reliably performing the behaviour 80 per cent of the time on command in various distracting locations, start to use variable reinforcement again and repeat step 9 in new locations. Challenge the dog's understanding of the behaviour.

Signs of Stress During Training

When you are training you need to watch out for various signs of stress. Stress can cause a lot of problems in your training. Yes, your dog needs to learn to work under some pressure, but pressure and stress are two different things. Stress can shut your dog down, sometimes indefinitely. Some dogs are more sensitive than others. Small things that seem insignificant to us may be a huge problem for a dog.

Here are some signs of stress to watch for:

- Licking lips
- Blinking excessively
- Pinning ears back
- Tucking the tail
- Running to the kennel
- Trying to leave the area

- Leaving the handler to get a drink of water
- Leaving the handler to go to the bathroom
- Having diarrhea
- Panting excessively
- Freezing
- Repeatedly taking a piece of equipment other than the one you want
- Becoming easily distracted
- Barking
- Spinning
- Sniffing
- Doing the zoomies (running around in large circles really fast with that tail-tucked-under look). Although this sometimes seems "cute" or funny, it is a sign that the dog has had too much and needs to blow off steam.

If the dog is leaving the handler to drink or relieve himself, it might seem to us that the dog is just thirsty or has to go to the bathroom, which may be the case if it happens only occasionally. But think about what happens when our dogs are drinking or relieving themselves. We leave them alone! So dogs that quit in the middle of a session for no reason to go and drink or piddle might be trying to get their handlers to leave them alone for a bit, ultimately relieving the stress.

A dog may become stressed because of the environment, the handler, or the behaviours he is being asked to perform.

People often interpret the dog taking other pieces of equipment as defiance, manipulation or independence. In my opinion, the dog is stressed because of the environment, the handler, or the behaviours he is being asked to perform. Taking other pieces of equipment is likely his strategy to try and release the pressure or please his handler by offering behaviours he has been highly reinforced for in the past. These are often pieces of equipment the dog does well and handlers conclude that the dog "wants to do his own thing." Actually he is trying to do something he thinks *you* like! He may be avoiding what you are asking (for many reasons) but he is trying to find another way to please you.

So next time your dog seems to blow you off, look very hard for stress issues that need to be addressed. A common cause of stress is making things too hard for the dog too soon. By forcing a dog to do something he is unsure of, you can damage the relationship you have worked so hard to build. And as the trainer of the dog, it is our responsibility to ensure we have given the dog time to feel secure on all equipment and with all the commands we wish to use.

There is also handler stress. Sometimes you will get stressed, annoyed, or impatient during training. Never let your dog see you this way. Take a deep breath and rethink your strategy. Are you asking too much? Is your timing off?

If I get to the point during training where I am so stressed I get angry or frustrated (and I have been there, we all have), it means my dog has proven he is smarter than I am. He has challenged me and I have not been able to rise to the challenge. I never want a dog to outsmart me and I will always rise to the challenge. I may need a time out and a drink first but I will rise to the challenge! So when I see people get angry or resort to yelling at their dogs in training or in a ring I always say, "There goes a smart dog and a not-so-smart trainer!"

Training Skills

There are some skills that you will develop the more you train. The better these skills are, the better a trainer you will be and the easier it will be to communicate with your dog. Keep these in mind and work on fine-tuning them as much as you can.

1. **Observation skills:** This is the ability to visualize beforehand what you want to reward and when you are training, see it and reward it!

2. **Mechanical skills:** This is the ability to get the food or toy to the dog quickly and be able to do it with either hand. Being able to throw a toy to a designated spot helps too.

3. **Record keeping:** Record keeping will enable you to know when to go back a step, when to stay where you are, and when to make it harder. Record keeping is a concept that I learned from Nancy Ouellette and Susan Garrett. It has been a huge eye-opener for me and for my students who now keep a record of their training in class. The idea of calculating and tracking your success rates to know whether or not your dog understands a concept seems simple, yet many people never do it. I understand that it is hard to keep a training log every time you go out to train; however, record-keeping can tell you:

   • how often the dog is getting reinforced: If your dog is shutting down, it's invaluable to have a record of how often you are giving a reward during your training. I see many people work their dogs over and over on something, trying to fix problems and then not rewarding when they finally get it right. Instead they just carry on. The poor dogs wind up going over and over the same skills with no idea of what is good, better, or best.

   • how many times he is successful compared to how many times he tried the exercise: This will tell you if you are asking the dog to do something that is too hard. If the number of unsuccessful attempts is much higher than the number of successful attempts, you may need to lower the level of difficulty for the dog.

   • if the dog understands the skill: By tracking the success rate over time you will see an increase (or possibly decrease) in your success rate. It is detailed information about what your dog understands and doesn't understand. This way, you cannot ignore or make assumptions about the behaviour because it is in black and white. Your records can tell you where to go next.

   • if the dog is sore or injured: A great example of record keeping making a huge difference is the story of Sheila and her Sheltie, Riley. As homework one week, Sheila had to track Riley's strides and times on a series of jumping patterns. We discovered through the record keeping that there was a considerable difference in striding when turning one direction versus the other. When we started to talk about this more, it came out that Riley had an injury some time back that Sheila thought was healed (just because a dog does not limp doesn't mean he is healed). In subsequent sessions, we took more notice of the way Riley moved. It turned out that Riley was actually still sore. It was the record keeping that made the difference for Riley and we were able to make some changes in his training program that made the sport more fun for him.

• understanding in new locations: I like to have my students track their results at their first trials and tell me details such as how many contacts were not performed as trained, how many weave pole entries were missed, how many bars were knocked, whether the mistakes were on turns or straight lines, and what the footing and weather were like.

It's important to find out if the dog is learning any patterns of behaviour in the ring. Sometimes handlers repeat obstacles in the ring to try to "fix" them. That often causes more problems. Some dogs learn to do the obstacles one way the first time and then do them correctly the second time. If this has become a pattern, the chain needs to be broken. The dog needs one chance to get it right and if he can't, then he needs to have a consequence. If the behaviour has not been trained or proofed properly, the dog should not be asked to do that piece of equipment in the ring.

Training Tip

Dogs go through learning curves just like people. One week your dog might be doing a great job on an exercise and the next week he'll act like he's never done it before in his life. Be prepared for that. Changes in distractions, environmental differences, body language, stress, and injury will all affect the learning curve. Be patient, use lots of praise and play, and don't be afraid to go back to the basics. Never allow yourself to get frustrated and give a negative or emotional correction.

Reinforcement

If you only read one chapter of this book, read this one. Knowing how to build and use reinforcement is what separates good dog trainers from brilliant dog trainers. Reinforcement is what drives the dog to perform the way you want. If your dog leaves you to visit other people or dogs, go sniffing in the grass, or try another piece of equipment, it is usually a simple reinforcement problem. The pot roast on the counter may reinforce your dog for doing some amazing agility maneuvers to get it, but the toy you're using for your training may not. This chapter will help you understand what reinforces your dog, and how to use those things to build other motivators that can be used in your training.

Key Concepts for Effective Reinforcement

Here are some key concepts around reinforcement that will help you become a better trainer. If you apply them, you'll see your dog begin to learn faster and your training will become more efficient.

1. Motivation

Many times when I teach there is a recurring theme amongst participants. How do I get my dog more motivated to work? It is a hard question to answer as every dog is different and the lifestyles people lead with their dogs are different. Often the dogs are not demotivated, they just lack understanding. Clearing up the confusion in their basic foundation skills and the handler's cue system helps. But there are a lot of dogs that can benefit from a bit of thought put into when you actually train. There are three things you need to be sure of when working with a dog that might be slightly under-motivated.

- **The dog should always be hungry.** Not just I-am-due-for-dinner hungry, but really bugging-you-for-food hungry. Even a skinny dog (that is otherwise healthy) that lacks motivation can afford to be put on a bit of a diet. If your dog ever turns his nose up at food, you are feeding him too much.

- **The dog should be bored.** This does not mean lying-on-the-couch-sleeping bored. I mean put the dog in a crate and have him hang out for awhile with nothing terribly interesting going on. When you want that dog to work he should be excited to get out of the boring old crate and do something with you! If he comes out and ignores you, he needs more crate time in his daily routine. This may take weeks to build up but it *will* happen and can change the dog's mindset into a more enthusiastic working partner.

- **The dog should be lonely.** In other words, if the dog has access to you every minute of the day, then you are not likely to be very exciting to him when you work. The dog needs down time in the crate so that he cannot necessarily demand attention from you whenever he feels like it. You want a dog that hangs on your every word, waiting for attention from you!

Now some people are just not willing to put Fluffy in a crate or on a diet, and that is okay. But be realistic about the kind of performance dog you will get. It's not about getting what you want; it is about wanting what you get. And if you are not willing to create the environment for your dog that encourages the kind of response to learning you want, then you need to accept the consequences and love the dog you have created.

2. Levels of Reinforcement

Having a variety of reinforcers allows the trainer to reward the dog at different degrees of performance. For example, when you are teaching the dog to sit, the next stage is to have the dog sit faster. If you say sit, and the dog does sit but it is very slow, what do you do? If you do not reward the dog, he may think he is supposed to do something else and you may lose the sit behaviour while the dog tries to figure it out. If you do reward, you are actually rewarding the slow sit. You can increase the level of reinforcement for the faster sits by rewarding the slow sit with praise or a piece of kibble and rewarding the faster sit with an enthusiastic game of tug or with five pieces of liver fed one after another.

The more types and levels of reinforcement you have in the toolbox, the better trainer you will be. The following chart gives some examples of different reinforcers:

Food Reinforcers	Toys	Action Games
Liver treats	Tug rope	Jumping up on you
Chicken	Frisbee	Tap the bum
Steak	Cow bonker	Praise
Wieners	Holey roller	Tag – tap and run
Cheese	Tennis ball	Belly rub
Kibble	Squeaky toy	Bum scratch

Figure out which reinforcers your dogs like best. Mine like chicken more than kibble, steak more than wieners, and liver above all else. As far as toys are concerned, the Frisbee and cow bonker are even, the tennis ball and squeaky come after the holey roller, and the tug toy is the ultimate. In the action games, the jumping up comes first, then the bum scratch, and then the rest. As a whole, my dogs like the Frisbee and tug toys the best, liver second, and jumping up third. Take the time to determine your dog's hierarchy and write it down.

3. Placement of Reinforcement

This is something that gets a bit technical but is very important. Where and how you deliver your reward significantly speeds up or slows down your training session. Think about delivering your reward in a place that will help your dog achieve the next step in training. An example is getting your dog to touch a plastic lid target in the centre. If you feed the dog to the right of the target all the time, the dog will shorten the behaviour and you will lose the nose touch. It will turn into a nose "swipe" at the side of the target so he can get to the cookie faster. If you feed too high, the dog will likely change the touch in the centre to a "swoop" or "scoop" and not actually touch the target. What happens between the click and the time the dog actually gets the reward is also teaching the dog something. In a sit-stay for example, getting up out of a sit to grab food is not something you want to reinforce. This will lead to the dog getting up to meet the handler out of most control positions, like the down on the table.

4. Random Reinforcement

Don't get yourself stuck with having to try to fool the dog into thinking you have food or a toy. Variable or random reinforcement just means surprising the dog with random rewards. If he does not always get the reward, he will learn to keep working and he will get the reward eventually. All final behaviours need to be put on a variable reinforcement schedule fairly quickly so that the dog can perform the behaviour without the food or toy reward every time.

Use of Conditioned Reinforcer

This is not a clicker training book, nor am I going to go into the concept of operant conditioning or other learning theories. It's important for good trainers to find out more about these things and how they apply to a training program. However, the one thing you must do is to make sure that you have established a "conditioned reinforcer" for your dog. This could be a clicker, a light for a deaf dog, or a word such as "Yes!" This marker must be paired with a primary reinforcer for your dog. This could be food, a toy, or both. Some trainers are good enough with their timing and observational skills that they can just place the reinforcement fast enough and so accurately that they don't need the verbal marker or clicker. But average trainers will be much more successful with a marker to help them identify what they are working on.

You will use your conditioned reinforcer to communicate with your dog. The sound or light will tell the dog what behaviour you want and what gets rewarded. The lack of the sound or light tells him not to waste any more time on that and to try something else.

Do not use agility equipment as a reinforcer for your dog. This will lead to huge problems in the ring later. Once in awhile I will use a piece of equipment to reinforce another piece of equipment only if the dog finds the first piece moderately stressful. I can count on one hand (not including my thumb) how many times I have had to do this! It is usually a last resort if shaping and using their primary reinforcers is not enough.

I use the word "Yes!" and a clicker. Personally, I find the clicker allows my dogs to learn much faster and with less frustration when I'm first training a behaviour. So I train all the physical attributes of the equipment with the clicker.

I do use the word "Yes!" to let the dog know he is correct once we have put the behaviour on stimulus control (in other words, named it) and we are chaining behaviours. By the time my dogs have named and are sequencing obstacles I very rarely use a clicker. I will bring it back out if a particular behaviour falls apart or if I need to define a specific part of the behaviour like nose touches, tight turns, or quicker downs on the table.

Use of Food in Training

One of the primary reinforcers for many dogs is, of course, food. The biggest problem is that food is often misused as a bribe or the dog is fed "just because." Here are some guidelines to help you use food properly:

- Use small, soft pieces about the size of your baby fingernail.

- Don't present food before the behaviour or to "get" a behaviour. If you think this may be happening, have someone watch you train, or videotape yourself training to see when and how you are using the food.

- Food should only be used to reinforce behaviour that has already happened, has been marked with a click or a "Yes!" and now needs to be rewarded.

- Use food for up-close or stationary behaviours like heeling, tables, downs, sits, stays, or behaviours you want to be repeated quickly, like targeting. Food is not a good reinforcer for distance work unless put into a food tube or food toy (see page 48).

- Establish levels of food reinforcers. Know which foods your dog enjoys, such as kibble, cereal, or carrots; foods your dog really likes such as cheese or hotdogs; and foods he will stand on his head for, such as steak or liver.

- Take into account how much food you use when you train. This has to come out of the daily feeding. There are some trainers who never feed their dogs a meal. All the food for the day is given in training.

- The dog should work for every piece of food.

- Know *why* you're giving each piece of food. Don't just feed the dog "because."

- Pay attention to what the dog is doing when he is actually eating the food. Whatever the dog is doing is what is getting reinforced. So if he stands up from his down-stay position to eat, standing is being reinforced, not the down!

Appropriate Amounts of Food

First, your dog must be hungry. If the dog is not hungry, he is either overweight or overfed. Dogs are the easiest creatures to put on a diet. I wish it were that easy for me! Most dogs today eat too much and too often. Obesity

One of the best ways to teach a food-motivated dog to play is to introduce a food toy.

is the number one health problem in most pet dogs. We see it in the agility ring as well, and it is unfortunate.

We can make the decision to run if we are packing a few extra pounds and everything hurts when we do those front crosses. Our dogs, on the other hand, don't get the opportunity to make those decisions. Overweight dogs will still try to run hard and fast. This can lead to injuries.

I don't recommend free feeding (when the food is left in the dish all day for the dog to eat at his leisure). Not only does it cause obesity, but free feeding also causes the handler to lose control of a very valuable reinforcer. If you leave the food down for the dog to pick and choose when he wants to eat, you will not be able to plan your training sessions because you'll never know when the dog is hungry.

The other reason I don't like students to free feed is that it is more difficult to tell if your dog is ill. When I put food down for my dogs, if any one of them won't eat I know instantly that there is something wrong and I watch that dog carefully for the next 24 hours.

If you can't easily feel your dog's ribs, put him on a diet. Start making him work for his dinner. Earning a meal could be something as simple as holding eye contact with you for five seconds. Don't feel guilty — dogs are genetically wired to have to work for their food. In the wild, animals have to work very hard for a meal. Earning his meal will help your dog be a better dog in the end.

Use of Play in Training

I use play for many, many things in agility training, not just to reward my dog for doing what I ask, but to teach impulse control, relieve stress, increase drive, and increase attention. It is also wonderful for rewarding the dog at a distance.

Dogs, from the time they are puppies, thrive on play. There are many ways to play with your dog that are reinforcing for him. There are tugging games using a rope toy or cow bonker; retrieving and chase games using a ball, squeaky toy or Frisbee; and physical games like "grab the feet," "tap the butt," wrestling, or jumping up on the handler. All of these are ways to reinforce the dog using something other than food.

Playing is about being able to turn your dog "on" and "off" whenever you want. Impulse control using a toy teaches the dog not to grab at the toy until it is offered, which is a skill I teach my dogs before we start any equipment training. All puppies should learn toy respect as part of their basic training:

"Give it," "Get it," and "Leave it" are important skills. This makes working with a toy in your hand a non-issue later. Also, controlling his urge to grab toys helps the dog later in his training to control his urge to "grab" obstacles.

Play is also a stress reliever for both the dog and the handler. When things go wrong in training and you know it is *you* and not the dog, and your dog knows something isn't right but doesn't know how to fix it, the toy can come in handy to relieve stress for both of you. Having a game of tug gives you time to think about what to do next to make the situation clearer for both of you.

In play, the toy acts as a reinforcer for distance work. The ability to throw the toy to the dog to mark and reward the behaviour of going out to an obstacle at a distance is a very handy tool. Most food-focused dogs do not work well at a long distance. That's because the reward is always coming from the trainer's hand, which is attached to trainer's body, and thus the dog has no reason to be away from the handler.

Dogs, from the time they are puppies, thrive on play.

How to Use Toys

Here are some principles to use when you're playing and reinforcing with toys:

- Work on a flat buckle collar only. Your dog should always have a collar on while training so you can gain control quickly.

- For a dog that runs off, keep the leash on when playing with the toy. The leash could be on the dog or on the toy – whichever is necessary.

- Only tug gently with young puppies until their teeth are developed. You can turn a dog off tugging if you try to tug hard when his mouth hurts, so let him do most of the pulling.

- Never tug harder or faster than the dog himself is tugging, try not to crank the dog's neck around, and keep the head low and make him use his rear end more than his front.

- Do not stuff the toy in the face of a dog that is not an avid tugger. Instead, drag the toy around on the floor, tap his butt or feet with it and tease him like you would tease a cat.

> **Criteria for a good toy:**
> - It fits in your pocket so you can hide it and surprise the dog.
> - The size is appropriate to the size of the dog you are working with.
> - It makes no noise.
> - You can throw it.
> - When you throw it, it doesn't roll, bounce or get lifted by the wind — you don't want the dog to injure himself.
> - You can play tug with it.
> - It has no handle that the dog could get caught or tangled in.

- Always quit before the dog wants to quit and never quit if the dog spits the toy out first. Try to get a couple of really good tugs and then ask him to release the toy.

- You start the game and you end game. Teach an experienced tugger to "take" and "give" the toy on command. No grabbing at the toy.

- Learn how to give a definite "presentation cue" to the dog with the toy that says, "Yes, you can grab it." If the toy is not "presented" to my dogs, they would not and should not grab it. I hold the toy out away from my body.

- Allow the new tugger to carry the toy around when you are done playing; the dog should be the winner in the end.

- Concentrate on associating the toy with you. You are trying to develop the dog's desire to play with you, not all by himself. Initially, use toys that the dog cannot run away with or put the toy on a line and reel the dog in.

- Use verbal praise when the dog is interacting with you and be quiet when he leaves. Be more enthusiastic when the dog puts his mouth on the toy; don't cheerlead to get him to get it and then quit praising when he does!

- Try not to pick up the toy if the dog drops it; try to get the dog to pick it up and bring it to you and then you make the "dead" toy come alive.

- You may have to get down to the dog's level to make him feel more comfortable.

De-stressing with play

I have found that playing is very important to dogs who show stress by getting higher and higher. When training gets more challenging for my red border collie, Sierra, she will often bark (or scream) at me and even try to bite me, neither of which I like my dogs to do.

Initially, when there was an error, I was stopping and withholding the reward. Then we would start again. This proved to make her more stressed. As a result, her ability to think and solve problems diminished.

My next step was to restart the sequence by looping her back over equipment to try again, thus maintaining the flow of the training time. The result was that she would start to loop back immediately on her own, even when I didn't want her to, without looking to me for information. I realized she actually wasn't trying to fix anything because the reinforcement of continuing to do equipment was fun. She had no idea there was an error. I had to find a way of letting her know that there was an error but still reward her to keep the stress level down.

Now when things go wrong, rather than stopping her, I call her in close to me to keep her off other equipment, and if she focuses on me instead of flinging herself into the closest tunnel, she gets the toy about 80 per cent of the time. The reward is for doing a side or close and not taking equipment on her own. Then we try the sequence again. This rate of reinforcement for attention on me keeps her calm enough to think, and I can withhold the toy on certain attempts to send a message.

- Don't be limited by the idea that a toy has to be something you buy in a store. Be creative! My puppies love paper towel rolls, socks, and plastic pop bottles.

- Put your hands on the dog during tugging: pat him, rub his face, tap him with your feet. (This is especially good for herding or terrier breeds that like to grab your feet when you are running.) This will get him used to people touching him, bumping weave poles, and other things he may run into while training and competing.

- Play beside you as well as in front. Have the dog drive in to your side for the toy, not always come in straight on.

For more info on how to get a dog to play, check out "Creating a Motivating Toy" by Susan Garrett at www.clickerdogs.com.

Games

This-one/That-one Game
Teach the dog to trade one toy for the other. Start with two identical toys. I tell my dog "get this one" and then play for a bit. While she is still tugging on toy number one, I pull out the other one and say "get that one" as I shake it and bang it on the ground beside her. I never take the first toy away; she needs to voluntarily drop the first toy and grab the second toy. Keep switching back and forth.

Turn
Tie a leash to the toy and throw it. When the dog grabs the toy, reel him in. You are trying to teach the dog to grab the toy and immediately turn back to you. This stops the dog from doing "laps" with toys.

Drive Back to Handler
Throw one toy and when the dog is on his way back to you, start running, or bring out a second toy. You want to teach the dog to drive into you for the toy. Use recall games and throw the toy between your legs, or have him chase you and catch you for a game of tug. This game is like a run-back in flyball.

Three-toy Retrieve

Throw one toy and let the dog pick it up, then call the dog and throw a second toy. The dog should drop the first toy and grab the second toy. When he brings the second toy back, throw the third toy between your legs. Run to the first toy, call his name and re-start the game. Each time you throw a new toy the dog should drop the first one. You just keep picking up the toys he drops. Sometimes get the dog to bring one toy in for a tug before you throw the other. It's great exercise for you and the dog!

Advanced This-one/That-one Game

Throw the first toy, and when he starts to bring it back, call his name and get him to drop the first toy and play with you with the second toy. He must leave the first toy alone while you play with toy number two. Move him away from the first toy as you play, then have him give you toy number two, and send him to pick up the first toy again. Call him and get him to drop the first toy again and play with the second one, as you continue to move around the room. Finally, send him back to the first toy by facing the direction of the toy to show the dog where it is.

Teaching an Older Dog or Food Motivated Dog to Play with Toys

Many of us started in this sport with an older dog that already had established patterns of behaviour. Many of them never played in relation to work. In 1992, when I started in competitive obedience, we did a lot of our training with food. My dog was highly motivated by food. My dogs all played, but not necessarily during their training.

Bounce loves her toys.

When I was trying to finish Piper's Agility Trial Champion of Canada title I ran into the age-old problem of the "Velcro dog" that couldn't do a Masters Gamble! I spent all winter teaching her to do distance work just using a food toy. She got her three Masters Gamble legs for her ATChC in the first three trials out after that winter.

So yes, there are certain breeds more prone to be food hounds than toy hounds. I have had Shelties all my life and even though they love to play, they are naturally inclined to work (and work well!) for food. Quite often we become highly reinforced by what our dogs do well and we are afraid to mess with it. It is a hard thing to spend six months working on getting your dog to play without doing much other training. Sometimes it takes that long and sometimes it doesn't. But even if it does, it is definitely worth the time!

I don't take any chances with my puppies. They all learn to play before we do any kind of formal training. I always go in knowing that it may take longer with one breed than another, but I never allow myself to blame the breed for the dog not tugging. Peak, my eight-month-old Sheltie puppy at the time I am writing this book, has done bits and pieces of things, mostly free-shaping exercises, but 90 per cent of her training has been encouraging her to play with me. I want her to be as crazy about the toys as my Border Collies are. It has taken longer to teach her this but she is a great tugger now!

I have been working on Peak's toy drive since I got her at 12 weeks old. She loved to pick things up and carry them around. I encouraged this and praised her for it. Sometimes it wasn't exactly something I wanted her to carry around (like underwear, my expensive Dita runners, or the hammer, measuring tape, and screwdriver while we were renovating). Quite often

My Dog Won't Play!

Pepper is a four-year-old Poodle cross who came to our training centre in January 2004. She was a rescue dog with separation anxiety. She was also a bit overweight and a bit shy. Her owner, Barb, brought her to classes only a few months after getting her. She responded instantly to the clicker and after the first six-week session she learned to settle in her crate during class and even relax if Barb left the room. Pepper didn't play in class at all but would play with a tennis ball or stuffed toy at home for short periods — she was not really what we would consider "toy motivated." Barb and Pepper enjoyed the classes and continued on with more training. When they began to work on their obstacle training for agility, it was obvious that Pepper needed to be convinced that a toy could be fun. Barb shaped her to tug and retrieve a "tug-and-treat" bag and also a "tug-and-toss" Frisbee. Now she will drive over jumps and through the weave pole chute to her toy and happily bring it back for a treat, ready to go again. Barb recently told us that the behaviour is starting to transfer to other toys at home and she is playing more and more. Sometimes, she even asks to play!

she will pick up a rock, or a crushed paper cup or even a piece of poop she finds outside as she goes out to potty. She carries it out, holds it and carries it back in where I promptly trade her for something I don't mind having in the house!

My philosophy is that dogs are dogs. Regardless of the breed, I expect them all to learn the same skills and I expect the same intensity in their desire to work with me. It is completely dependant on how much time, energy and patience I put into their training. I will not make excuses for breed or temperament. I have seen some incredible work from breeds that you would not consider naturally driven. And it all depends on the experience and dedication of their owners. Of course, some dogs will take longer to develop their play drive but if you can train a dog to do something as unnatural as weave poles, you can certainly train a dog to do something as natural as play! Don't make excuses as to why the dog won't play, just get to work teaching the dog that playing is fun too!

There are many ways to teach a food-motivated dog to play. Most take time and consistency and a bit of creativity on the owner's part. One of the best ways is to introduce a food toy. There are different types of food toys. Here are some of the ones we have used.

- **Food Tubes:** These are plastic tubes filled with food that the dog can retrieve back to the handler for a cookie.

- **Tug 'N' Treat Bags:** These are soft tug toys filled with treats that the dog can tug on as well as retrieve.

- **Plastic Container:** I used a film container and taught Piper that there is food in it and that I will open it and give her a treat from it if she brings it back to me when I throw it. Use for small dogs only. Labs will just eat the whole container!

- **Modified Toys:** I have also used a tennis ball with a slice cut in it. I filled the ball with treats and used it the same way as the film container.

Food Tubes are plastic tubes filled with food that the dog can retrieve back to the handler for a cookie.

- **Food Sock:** Susan Garrett has written about what she calls a food sock. It is a sock with a chicken wing in it. This will entice the dog to grab the sock and pull. You can use this to get the initial spark to chase the food started. Of course, never let the dog get the sock away from you, especially if you have a Lab — you don't want them to eat the sock along with the chicken wing!

All of these will work if you don't give in to the dog and do all the work yourself. For example, you throw the food toy and your dog runs out and then stops and just looks at it. What do you do? If you always go out to the dog and open the toy and either throw it again or feed him he has trained you to retrieve the toy. Here are the steps to work through:

1. Feed all meals from the toy. The toy needs to be big enough for the dog to eat out of.

2. Open the food toy, give him a chance to chow down a few treats, and then take it away. Repeat until the food is all gone. Don't touch the food with your hands in any way.

3. Start to put the toy on the ground full of food. If the dog pushes it or noses it or paws at it, open and feed some of his meal. Close it again, put it back on the ground, and repeat.

4. Once he is instantly going to the toy when it is dropped, try to get him to pick it up for the food. If he picks it up off the ground, click, open the toy, and feed. Drop it again.

5. Continue to drop the food toy and have the dog pick it up, but expect the dog to move the toy towards you. If he just picks it up and drops it, simply sit in a chair and wait. If he is hungry he will find a way of getting that toy to you!

6. Once he will pick it up and bring it to you, start to throw it farther away. Don't throw too far too soon. If the dog is only mildly hungry, and you throw too far, the energy efficient part of him could take over and decide it is too much energy to go out that far!

7. Once you have him retrieving the food toy at any distance, start racing him to it. If you get there first, he doesn't get the treats! Let him win more often than he loses. Make a great game of grabbing the toy and running away from him and get him to chase you with it to open it. Have fun and be exciting and unpredictable. Dogs love that!

8. After the dog will do the above reliably, I start to get him to bring it to my hand. He is not allowed to drop it on the ground any longer. If the dog drops it, I wait with an outstretched hand. At first I will take any attempt to get it in my hand and may even move the hand under the toy to catch it so that I can reward.

9. The next step is to get the dog to hold it while I tap or touch it. If he lets it drop, he has to pick it up again. Because dogs are energy efficient, they will quickly figure out that the fastest route to the cookies is to keep that thing in his mouth!

10. After I can tap and touch the toy with the dog holding on to it, I start to give a little tug. If the dog holds it, I click and treat. If the dog lets go, I step back and get him to bring it to me again.

Once I can do a small tug, I gradually increase the intensity of the tug, and expect the dog to tug back until I click. If, at any time, he drops it before I click, I also drop it and the dog has to start over by picking up the toy and getting it to me again. The dog realizes it's a big waste of energy to let go before that click!

Once I can do a small tug, I gradually increase the intensity of the tug, and expect the dog to tug back until I click.

In the beginning, any interest in playing with toys should be praised and encouraged. As the dog is learning to play with a toy, try not to call him off, or correct, for picking up any toy. Even if the dog runs around an obstacle in training to grab the toy, don't worry about it. Of course, it's hard to be enthusiastic at 11 p.m., which is when Peak seemed to want to play the most!

When I started teaching Peak to play with toys, it had to be done when she was in the most playful mood. I could get her to play at other times but not with the intensity and joy I wanted her to have. I did not like practicing playing when she was giving me less than intense interest. She seemed happiest to play between 9 p.m. and 11 p.m. It wasn't ideal for me after teaching all day, but if that was when she was keen, that was when we played! Since I invested so much time in building her play drive, I can now ask for it anytime and get the intensity I want.

Pre-agility Obedience

If you have never taken a basic obedience class, I suggest that you find one with a good instructor who understands the use of positive reinforcement in training and knows something about agility.

Our basic obedience students that have agility in their future plans start their training slightly differently than our pet or competition obedience people. For example, we teach future agility competitors the ability to work equally on the right side and the left side. And we talk about the importance of play. All of our students work with a clicker to train new behaviours.

Equipment You Will Need

Here is a list of equipment we recommend you have when you start training agility:

- Flat-buckle collar

- Six-foot leash

- Crate (and a crate-trained dog)

- Good pair of running shoes

- Plexiglass target

- Wiffle ball or "Ally Oop"

- Two-foot by three-foot mat

- Lots of toys the dog loves, preferably tug toys, but also those that you can throw for distance work

- Good variety of treats that are soft and small

Basic Foundation Skills

The following exercises are simple and are great life skills, as well as being basic skills for your training "tool box" before you embark on your agility training career.

Eye Focus

Teach the dog that making eye contact gets him cookies. Hold a piece of food in front of the pup's nose — make sure he sees the cookie — then slowly move it out to the side. When the pup looks away from the food, click and treat. Do not say a word. Initially, reward the dog for looking anywhere but at the food. Later, build up to having the dog look into your eyes. Then you can build up duration of the eye contact, and also add in distractions.

We do the eye focus game and a lot of our initial obedience exercises with hand signals first. This helps young and distracted dogs focus on their

Show the puppy a piece of food and move it to the side.

When the pup looks away from the food, click and treat.

handlers in a class or training environment. They learn that if they look around at other people and dogs instead of at the handler they will miss something they could have earned a cookie for. They need to watch the handler for the hand signals that produce the cookie. So we do eye focus first, and then the sit and down on hand signals initially. Then we add in the verbal commands later.

Walk, Stop and Look

I like this exercise as it helps the dog to automatically look back at you when you stop moving. Just walk around with the dog on leash. When he is looking at something else, stop moving. Be ready to click when the dog looks back at you. Feed close to your legs. Initially you are just clicking the head turn and later add eye contact with you. Never step towards the dog to feed. Make the dog come to you.

Sit and Down

There are many ways to teach these two basics. I always teach the sit and down with a hand signal first with puppies because it means that they must be looking at me to get the signal, which gives them the opportunity to earn the click and treat. This follows the "walk, stop and look" exercise nicely, as the dog has already been conditioned to automatically look at me. When the dog is reliably looking back at me every time I stop, and will respond to the sit and/or down hand signal, I make the criteria more difficult by only rewarding when the dog responds within one second of seeing the signal. Pretty soon the dog is sitting or going down almost before the signal. This is when I tag on the command for sit or down just before the hand signal. Works like a charm!

Walk, stop and look: Be ready to click when the dog looks back at you.

Wait/Leave it

I like this way of teaching a "wait" as it teaches a "leave it" as well and requires the dog to control his natural urge to grab for his own reinforcement.

Place 10 pieces of food on the floor about two feet in front of the dog. Show the dog that the food is there, then quickly put your hand over the food. Let him have a go at trying to get the food out from under your hand. When he finally gives up and backs away, quickly feed him from the pile. If he gets up to dive on the food once it is uncovered, simply cover it up again. You have to be very quick when you start to feed. Feed high to keep the dog's head up and away from the food. As long as the dog holds position, keep feeding until all the food is gone. If the dog moves forward at any time, quickly cover the food again so he can't get it. Wait for the dog to reposition himself back to where he was when he was getting the treats (this could be a sit, down or stand as long as he moves away from the food).

It is okay if the dog tries to move. That is how he will figure out that no reward is forthcoming if he chooses that behaviour. Say "okay" and release to play with the dog when all the food is gone off the floor. Puppies learn this very quickly and it is very cool to see 12-week old puppies learn to back up and reposition themselves.

Build up to being able to place the treats on the ground and walk around, feeding every few seconds if the dog holds position. This can be done with the dog's dinner, toys, and other objects the dog really wants.

Sit signal: Start by showing the dog the food.

Raise your hand straight up to your shoulder.

Get it/Give it

Once the dog understands the "wait/leave it" game, you can start to use your toys in the same fashion. Place the toy on the ground in front of the dog. When the dog backs away or holds his position, click and say "Get it!" Have a great game of tug with the dog.

When it is time to give up the toy, you can simply say, "Give it," or whatever word you want to use, and stop tugging. Don't let go, just make the toy boring. If you try to pull the toy out of the dog's mouth, you're continuing the game as far as the dog is concerned. Click and treat when the dog gives it up.

For dogs who don't want to give up their toy, I just hold the collar up under the chin and wait them out. Hold the toy lightly, and don't respond to any effort on the dog's part to keep tugging. Do not make eye contact and do not talk. I have yet to find a dog that won't give the toy up eventually with this method.

Incorporate your sits and downs with the "get it/give it" game. Start with a tug game, say, "Give it, sit," then click and play tug again. Do the same for the downs. Make it fun for the dog to do sits and downs.

Back Up

We generally shape this behaviour from a sit. Once the dog will offer a sit, we wait until the dog stands out of the sit or shuffles his rear-end around a

---

Keep Trying

You and your dog will have training sessions when the exercise is a tough one and both of you are trying very hard to get it right but something keeps going wrong. If the dog goes for too long without reinforcement for something, he will become frustrated and may bark, spin, jump up or even quit working altogether. This means your rate of reinforcement has become so low you have shut your dog down. We use the "keep-trying" exercises to keep the dog motivated to work when things get tough. Hand targets are a great way to get the dog back working with you. A simple sit or down or a trick like spin right or left will also act as a keep-trying exercise. Anytime you feel the rate of reinforcement has dropped too low just ask for one of your keep-trying exercises and this will help the dog to stay working with you.

You can also use the hand target as a check-in on a walk: if the dog comes running towards you, hold out your hand for the touch, and when you get it, click and treat, then send the dog off to play again. This way, coming to you is rewarding and does not automatically mean the end of the walk.

---

bit and click that behaviour. Once the dog understands it has something to do with his rear he will usually stand. Once we have shaped the sit to the stand, we start to click for back feet moving any direction. Then we start to require the back feet to move back. We generally watch the back feet, not the front, because if we start to click front feet then we wind up with the dog waving and high fiving. We really want the dog to understand that it is about the back feet.

Another way to teach back up is to lure the dog between the couch and coffee table with a cookie, feed, and then remove the food and wait. The dog will likely try to back up out of the space. Click or say, "Yes!" and feed. Then have the dog come in close to you so he can back up again.

You can also use the "wait/leave it" exercise. Hold out your hand with a treat in it. When the dog comes to investigate the treat, simply close your hand and wait. The dog will probably give you a nose bump or paw at your hand. When he gets nothing for that, he will likely stop and think about what to do to get that cookie and then back off your hand. When he moves away from your hand, click and open your hand for him to have the treat. Try again and he will probably back off the treat a little quicker. Once he is taking a step away from the food, click! As you reward him for backing off the food, he will likely come back in and then give you a stronger or more exaggerated back up motion. Click! Work until he is backing up one step, then two steps, then three steps, and so on. Try to keep him backing up in a straight line.

Stand

I like my dogs to have a pop-back stand rather than having them walk forward into a stand. I teach the stand after I have taught the dog to back up from a sit. When the dog will pop his rear-end up to back up, I click early and reinforce the pop up to the stand. It teaches a lovely stand in which the dog uses his rear end.

Hand targets are a great foundation skill for puppies and new dogs.

Hand Targets

Hand targets are a great foundation skill for puppies and new dogs. They can be used as a "keep trying" exercise, and to refocus the dog back to you.

Hold out your left hand. Most dogs will immediately investigate it. Click and feed for any interest in your left hand. When you reward, put the food in or in front of your left hand. Increase the criteria until the dog will push his nose into the palm of your hand. Do not give it a command; let your hand be the cue. If you are having trouble, put a piece of food in between the fingers of your left hand and use it as a lure. When the dog touches, instead of feeding him the piece between your fingers, transfer a treat from your right hand into your left hand to reward. Use the lure three times only, then go back to shaping. Teach a right-hand touch as well.

Say Hello

This exercise tells the dog that he has permission to go see a particular dog or person. Have the dog on leash. Wait for eye contact, and when you get it, release the dog to see the other dog or person. This way, the dog is polite and you can avoid potential problems. After the greeting, expect the dog to come back to you.

Don't let your dog rush into a strange dog's face. Many excited puppies have run into the face of the wrong adult dog and paid for it. Sometimes that experience stays with them for life. I never send my dogs to someone or something I don't know or that may hurt or scare them. Therefore, when they hear "go say hello" they automatically think they know the person or dog and greet in an appropriate way.

Recalls

A reliable recall is one of the most important skills you can have. Calling your dog is a defining moment in your relationship with him. If your dog will not come when he is called, how likely will he respond to commands on an agility course? The recall is also the easiest exercise to sabotage.

Here are some do's and don'ts for recalls:

DO'S:
- Do praise and reward the dog every time he comes when called.
- Do be consistent with one command such as "here," "to me," or "come."
- Do keep the recall game fun, fun, fun! Do everything in your power to keep that dog wanting to come to you no matter what. Hold his

interest by clucking like a chicken, doing cartwheels, standing on your head, whatever it takes. Engage your dog in your antics.

- Do conduct lots of restrained recalls between two people with a reward for every time the dog comes.

- Do practice calling your dog for a treat and then release him to go and play again. Always let him have one or two more romps once you put the leash on him to go home. If you just put the leash on and go home, the leash will become a cue for the game to end. Then the dog will learn to avoid you when you have the leash in your hand.

- Do teach your dog to come to other people when he is called by his name. This could be a potential lifesaver!

DON'TS:
- Don't call a dog to you to administer unpleasant things like clipping toenails or bath time. If you need to do any of these things go and get the dog.

- Don't call your dog to punish him. Even if you are so mad you could throttle him, if he comes to you with total trust, do not hurt him in any way, shape or form. As much as you would like to, this will do irreparable damage to your recall, not to mention your relationship with your dog. Try to think ahead. Are the future consequences worth punishing the dog at that moment? At that point the punishment is for you to let out anger. It absolutely does not teach your dog anything positive.

- Don't practice the recall exercise off leash with an inexperienced or uncontrollable dog. If you choose to remove the leash, don't be surprised if the dog won't come when you call him. It will leave you completely powerless. Without a leash, you have no way to enforce your command, so don't bother using it. Just run the other way and make it a game. Praise when the dog does come to you. When going from on-leash recalls to off-leash recalls, do so in a controlled environment with little or no distractions and in an enclosed area (i.e: a backyard with a fence). You can gradually work up to the football field. Each time you change the environment or the outside distractions, put the dog back on leash and do some controlled on-leash recalls first. A good time to practice recalls is when your dog is happiest to see you such as when you get home from work.

Foundation Work

There are many easy training activities you can do with your puppy or beginner agility dog to build foundation skills. Most are more than just great agility basics; they are games your dog will enjoy for the rest of his life. My dogs will still go stand on a block or small stool, nose touch a hand or touch a wiffle ball that gets left out on the floor. These were skills that they learned early on and they still find them fun. I incorporate many ground-work skills in my day-to-day play with the dogs. They never get the ball or Frisbee until they perform some kind of foundation behaviour first. This approach keeps the basics from getting boring and helps to reinforce foundation work for the rest of the dog's life.

Rear End Awareness

As with any sport, there are risks involved in playing agility, and it requires dogs to be in very good shape. This is especially important for certain breeds of dogs with structures that may not be ideal for the sport. One of the things that will help your dog immensely with many different aspects of agility is to understand how to use his rear end. Many dogs do not know how to use their rear end to their advantage.

I had always thought that there was more to teaching a dog to jump than what we generally did in agility. We concentrated a lot on our handling skills and directional skills on jumps, but no one really talked about teaching a dog the mechanics of jumping.

Then I was lucky enough to attend one of Susan Salo's jump clinics. Susan Salo spent 35 years immersed in the world of horse jumping and has brought her experience to the agility world. It was like a light went on for me and the answers I was looking for appeared right before me. What really amazed me was how far my own dogs had come in the sport without a single clue about how to jump!

The thing that my dogs were lacking, and that is missing in most dogs I see in the ring, is knowledge of how to use their rear ends. Susan Garrett has written many articles on various rear end awareness exercises and I can't tell you how important they are for the dogs. They really opened my eyes to how dogs move.

During the clinic it became painfully obvious that many of the dogs were in the same predicament as mine. The skills Susan was asking these experienced agility dogs to do seemed very simple to us but the dogs had a very hard time executing them without some knowledge of how to use their rear ends.

Start by shaping the dog to put his front feet on a low stool, phone book or stack of rubber mats cut into a 10-inch by 10-inch square.

With my dance background, I liken rear-end work to the simple movement a young dancer learns at his or her first ballet class, the "demi plie." It is simply bending the knees with two-thirds of your weight over your toes. Sounds simple right? Well, dancers do demi plies their entire careers! It is a foundation skill for a dancing career. Dancers who never master it don't succeed. And dancers who don't have a good demi plie can't jump.

In the same way, dogs need to learn the basic skills of rocking their weight onto their rear ends and being aware of using their back feet. Dogs are naturally inclined to "pull" themselves over and through things instead of pushing with their rear ends. If we never show them that they can use their rear ends, and that it is actually easier than pulling, the result will be too much front-end strength and weak rear muscles.

Therefore, it's important to start our new dogs and baby dogs on the following fun and educational rear-end awareness exercises.

Stool Work

We use this exercise in our classes for two reasons. First, the exercise helps handlers practice their shaping skills so they can learn to shape — rather than lure — the dog to get on the stool. Secondly, it is excellent for building-rear end awareness. It helps with agility skills such as jumping, contacts, and weave pole entries, not to mention 360-degree turns in rally obedience and left turns in traditional obedience.

Start by shaping the dog to put his front feet on a low stool, phone book or stack of rubber mats cut into a 10-inch by 10-inch square. It doesn't need to be tall: six inches high is great for young puppies or toy breeds, and for

Once the dog is happily putting both feet on the stool on his own, try to get him to move his back feet around the stool.

older puppies or adults dogs, eight to 10 inches high is suitable.

Once the dog is happily putting both feet on the stool on his own, try to get him to move his back feet around the stool. This will isolate the use of the dog's back feet as opposed to using all four feet. The front feet should stay on the stool as he moves around. With all our puppies doing this at once, our class looks a bit like a circus dog act!

Back Up

Have the dog back up on stairs, between your legs, through a ladder, on the left side of you, and on your right side. These are all great strengthening and pre-jump exercises for dogs' rear ends. Instructions for teaching a back up are in chapter four on page 58.

Jump Bumps

Susan Salo uses these in her jump clinics and they are wonderful. They are pieces of large PVC, about four inches, eight inches and 10 inches in diameter, cut in half so that they resemble speed bumps. We use them in our classes for teaching the dogs to rock back before they go into a sequence of jumps. They can be used in a line or in a circle and they should be kept very close together to encourage the dogs to "bounce" through them. You want the dogs to learn to pick up their feet and not hit them or step on them. The nice thing about jump bumps is that if the dogs do step on them, they don't roll on the ground like jump bars do so there are no safety issues.

Ladder Work

Some large dogs have trouble with the teeter totter and dogwalk because they can't figure out how to keep their back feet on the narrow ramps. Good, old-fashioned ladder work is great for teaching them to figure out how to keep their back feet underneath them. Simply build or use a ladder

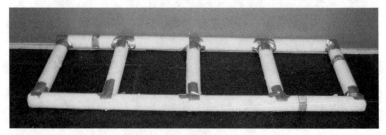

For the puppies we made a ladder out of Styrofoam pool noodles. We just cut them and duct taped them into the shape of a ladder.

that lies on the ground and have the dogs step through the rungs. Do this on leash and don't rush them through it — let them pick their own speed. For the puppies we made a ladder out of Styrofoam pool noodles. We just cut them and duct taped them into the shape of a ladder. They are small, portable and the pups can't bang soft bones on them.

Targets

Targets are used throughout our training program. Targeting is one of the foundation behaviours our dogs learn as puppies. Eventually it is used for more advanced work such as contacts, distance work and practicing shaping skills.

A target is in fact a lure, but it is not trained with a lure. I believe that targeting should be trained as a behaviour in itself. The dog touches the target and receives a reward.

I do not believe in open food targets, or food lying on a lid. Putting food on the target is luring and it doesn't teach the dog that what we really want is for him to touch the target without food on it. They just learn to run to anything that looks like a target on the ground and sniff for food.

We also don't put a verbal cue on the target for a long time, as the presence of the target should mean touch it. So if you do not want your dog touching the target or wiffle ball, do not leave them lying around. If a target is left out and the dog runs to touch it, reward, and pick up the target immediately. If you have no cookie to reward it, simply praise and then pick it up.

We shape the dogs to touch the following different kinds of targets.

Hand Targets

Hand targeting is used for all sorts of things in agility and dog training in general. It is one of the foundation exercises in our puppy classes. We use it to help people with their clicker timing as they can feel their dogs touch their hands (see page 60).

Hand targeting can also be used as a "check in" on walks. When you are out walking with the dog, hold out your hand as he runs towards you. If the dog sees it and chooses to come in and touch your hand, jackpot with something really tasty, then send the dog off to play again. This encourages the dogs to check in often without fear of being put back on leash.

Using a hand target is also a great tool for positioning dogs in heel position or beside the handler. In obedience, hand targets can help teach finishes and automatic sits.

If your dog is distracted or confused and you are losing his attention, doing a hand target can get him back. If you have run into a roadblock in training and your rate of reinforcement needs to be increased, you can use a hand target so that the dog can be rewarded before he starts to work again. Mixing up rewards for hand targeting by sometimes playing tug after the target and sometimes giving a cookie keeps things interesting for the dog. It's good for the dog to learn that not everything is always followed by food.

Lid Targets

Using a margarine lid or plexi glass target, we shape the dogs to touch it first in our hand and eventually down on the floor. They must touch with their nose, not their feet. Ideally we want a firm bop in the centre of the target. Once the behaviour is strong, we transfer the target to the ground between their feet, and eventually, to the end of the contact equipment.

We use hand targets to help people with their clicker timing as they can feel their dogs touch their hands.

We teach the dogs to touch the wiffle ball with their noses.

Wiffle Ball/Alley OOP

The wiffle ball is just a ball on a stick. We teach the dogs to touch it with their noses. Eventually, they learn to go to it from a distance. We work up to a 30-foot send to the wiffle ball. The wiffle ball helps train the dog to do a piece of equipment without the handler, because it acts as a focal point for the dogs. It keeps them moving in a straight line, and stops them from being concerned about the equipment as they are more focused on the wiffle ball. We fade the wiffle ball by moving it farther away until it is no longer needed.

Rally Obedience

Rally obedience is a relatively new dog sport and we have found it to be a fabulous addition to our agility program. It is basically agility flatwork set up as a numbered course. The exercises are fun, challenging, and great for teaching the dog to work in close. There are also a lot of exercises that require good rear end awareness and work on both the right and left sides. The Association of Pet Dog Trainers (www.apdt.com), the American Kennel Club (www.akc.org) and Canadian Association of Rally Obedience (www.canadianrallyo.ca) are some rally associations.

Distance and Directional Commands

Someone once told me that agility is won or lost on the ground between the obstacles. This is 100 per cent true. Training is getting so good, most competitive dogs have great contacts and weave poles. What is important is how quickly and accurately you can get your dog from one piece of equipment to the other. The following are commands we use between the obstacles that come in very handy.

Right and Left

I start by teaching my puppies to spin right or left on a verbal command on the ground. I think this helps them to understand that their bodies can go in two different directions and that they can be asked for one or the other on command. Many dogs are right or left sided, just as people are right or left handed, so the dog may favour one direction when you teach right and left. It is important to remember that teaching right and left has many stages and takes many repetitions.

1. Start with the dog facing you. Lure the dog in a circle with a cookie. Put the cookie in front of his nose and get him to follow it around in a circle. Try to get the dog's nose to move towards his hip as he turns. Do this until he is chasing the cookie around fairly quickly. Do not name it yet. I use my right hand to turn the dog to his left and my left hand to turn the dog to his right.

2. Try it without the cookie by holding your hand as if the cookie is there. Click and treat when the dog is finishing the spin.

3. Start to use just a finger motion and click and treat. Note: The motions of the hand signals are like the two halves of the letter W. Put your right finger in the centre of the W and draw the right loop down and then up. This is the motion of my hand signal for the dog to turn left. Do the opposite with the left hand for the right turn.

4. When you can get the dog to spin both ways on finger signals, start to name the behaviours. Say the verbal command "right" or "left" and then give the hand signal. Remember, you're naming the dog's right and left, not yours.

Put the cookie in front of his nose and get him to follow it around in a circle.

5. Make the hand signal smaller and smaller until you fade it completely and the dog will spin on the verbal alone.

6. Although it seems as though the dogs understand "right" and "left," the dog has actually learned what I call the "this way/that way" game: if it isn't "this way" then it must be "that way." They usually do not have a clear understanding that the word applies to the direction they spin. So if you say "right" and the dog goes left, and you don't reward, he will likely offer you the other direction the next time.

7. The next step is to teach the dog that the word before the spin is actually telling him something. So if you say "right" and the dog spins left, rather than saying right again, say "left." The dog will likely go to the "this way/that way" game and offer the opposite of what he did the first time. (Which in this case would be right.) When he doesn't get rewarded for that one either, he will become confused as the "this way/that way" rules don't work any more. It's usually at this point that dogs start to figure out that the word before the spin is the key to the cookie.

Here is an example of a training session you might have at this stage:

Verbal cue	What dog does	Reward
Right	Dog turns left	No
Left	Dog turns right	No
Left	Dog turns left	Yes
Left	Dog turns left (that is the last thing he got rewarded for — I want to keep the rate of reinforcement as high as possible)	Yes
Right	Dog turns left	No
Right	Dog turns right (reverting to this way/ that way game)	Yes (to keep him working)
Left	Dog turns right	No
Right	Dog turns left	Wait and don't say anything dog eventually turns right reward! Jackpot if you like and quit for the day

During this stage you may get the dog reverting back to previous behaviours, barking at you for changing the rules of the game, jumping up and giving any number of stress-relieving behaviours. Just work through it and keep the rate of reinforcement as high as you can while keeping the dog learning.

Initially you can also try shaping the spin. This is more difficult but is a great exercise in shaping. It will challenge you as a trainer and make you get creative with your placement of reinforcement.

Out and Away

These are the two directional commands I use for distance work with my dogs. Each has its own unique meaning. I used to train only the "out" command, but when I started training my second Border Collie, I did such a great job of the "out" on a verbal alone, that I found when I tried to use it multiple ways with my body he just didn't understand.

The first distance behaviour, my "out" command, means make a sharp 90- or 180-degree turn away from me and take the next thing you see. The end result is that we will be going in the opposite direction with you on my other hand. It's basically a rear cross at a distance.

The other behaviour, my "away" command, means move forward and laterally away from me but stay on the same side. It does not mean take the next obstacle you see, it means keep moving to the side until you hear an

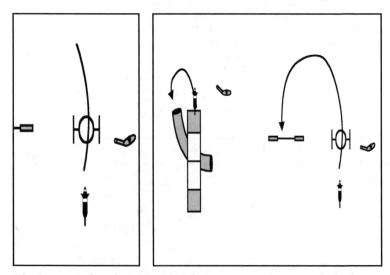

"Out" means make a sharp 90- or 180-degree turn away from me and take the next thing you see.

obstacle command. The two behaviours are very different.

However, both behaviours are dependant on the dog being able to see me or know what side of me he is on. Neither will work if I am directly behind the dog.

Out: Once you have taught your right and left commands you can use them to teach out. Start with the dog beside you facing the same way as you are. Say, "Out!" and give your directional cue that will turn the dog away from you. If the dog is on your right side the command would be "out, right." When the dog turns, you turn with him and step in behind. The dog should now be on your left and you will both be facing 180 degrees the other direction. Repeat on the left. You and the dog turn the same way. Work until you can drop the "right" and "left" commands and the dog will turn on the "out" command. Always place the reward away from you by throwing a toy.

Once the dog will do this on your right and left, start walking with the dog beside you and give the command. Then try it at a jog, and then at a run.

Away: I start teaching "away" on the flat using trees in the yard or park or a post in our training centre. You can also use a chair, jump standard, pylon or anything your dog can go around.

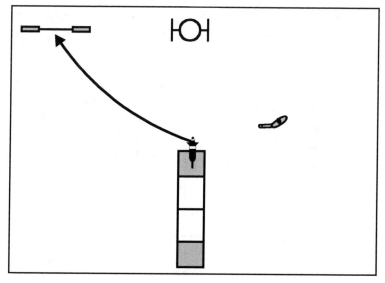

"Away" means move forward and laterally away from me but stay on the same side.

Start by shaping or luring the dog around something (a chair, coffee table, post, jump standard). You are not allowed to go around the object with the dog. The dog should start on your right and move away from you to go around the object in a counter-clockwise direction. From your left, your dog will go clockwise. (This is simular to "away to me" and "come by" in sheep herding.)

Start to move farther and farther away from the object. Add your "away" command using an extended arm signal to hold the dog out. When you have worked up some distance from your dog, you should be rewarding by throwing a toy. I then transfer this to a curved tunnel. I use "away" and step laterally to get the dog to take the further tunnel entrance.

Other Useful Commands

Look Back/Go Back

Put the dog in a sit or down and ask him to wait while you place a toy or his dinner dish on the ground behind him. Walk back out and stand in front of him. When he looks at you and not at the toy or food, release with a "Look back!" command. I will also add in "get it" after they do actually look back so they know they can have the toy/or food. Because I do not release until the dog looks at me, this is also a great focus exercise. Initially I will take eye contact even if there is an ear twisted back towards the toy. Later, I want full attention: ears forward and focus on me before I release.

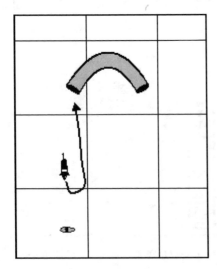

Turn

"Turn" should eventually mean that if the dog is running in a certain direction, he should turn around and go the other way. It doesn't matter which direction the dogs turns; he is free to choose.

I teach "turn" using a Frisbee or toy the dog likes. I throw the

You can use your "look back" command to help the dog find an obstacle behind him.

toy a few times until the dog is anticipating the toy and running out ahead of me. Then I start to throw but stop as the dog runs out. I say "turn" and the dog's name. When the dog stops, turns and looks at me, I click and throw the toy directly to him.

The next step is to get the dog to turn away from me. I put the dog in a sit-stay, do a recall, then say, "Turn" and throw the toy behind the dog.

"Turn" can be a great way to make your "away" around a tree fun. Send your dog around the tree, and when he come towards you tell him, "turn" and have him go back around the other way.

Always reward the dog by throwing the toy directly to him. He shouldn't creep in to you for the reward. He should know to stay where he is as the reward will be coming to him. If the dog creeps, I always throw the toy behind him, never between me and the dog, or he will want to get closer and closer to me.

Moving Wait

I know it sounds like a contradiction, but I want my dogs to be able to be moving at a full out run and stop in their tracks on a "wait" command. They should stop where they are and wait for another command. I teach it the same way as I teach "turn," only I say "wait" and I don't expect any turn except for the dog to look at me. You can also teach it with a recall, then step in with a hand up and say wait. When the dog hesitates, click and throw the toy. You don't want any creeping forward on the "wait."

I use this command for tough directionals out of tunnels because the

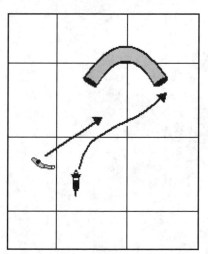

dogs tend to come out fast and wide. "Wait" means stay at the end of the tunnel (or wherever you were told "wait") and listen for a new command.

Use "away" and step laterally to get the dog to take the further tunnel entrance.

Flatwork

Someone once said, "Agility is won or lost on the ground between the obstacles." How fast and smoothly you get your dog from one obstacle to the other is what will make the difference between first place and second place. Flatwork is all about transitions. How well you transition your dog from one obstacle to the next depends on how much work you actually do on the ground without equipment. Many people watch agility and all they can see is the equipment performance. What they don't see is all the work it takes to keep the dog off the equipment when he isn't supposed to be on it! Think about how much reinforcement you use to get your dog to perform equipment. There will be lots of value built into the equipment and your dog will naturally gravitate to where he gets reinforced. Flatwork is about making sure your dog finds not taking equipment as reinforcing as taking it. Running with you can be as much fun as jumping or weaving.

Try running with your dog beside you. Does he run out in front and try to stop you? Does he run behind you and try to nip your feet? Does he jump up and try to grab your arm? Does he run out in front looking for a toy or sniffing? These are all behaviours that are completely natural for the dogs to do but will not help you on an agility course. Flatwork training will help your dog learn to run beside you in control on both your right and left sides, turn towards and away from you, and drive out in front. When your dog can run a full course on the ground with no equipment, complete with turns, crosses, stops and starts, doing a course with equipment will be no problem at all.

Side or Close

The first skill required is a "side" or "close." This simply means that the dog can run along beside the handler, on cue, and not take any other equipment, jump up, bite or grab at the handler in any way. The dog is completely focused on the handler. Many dogs cannot run beside their owners. What is the sport of agility all about? It is running with the dog!

Start teaching "side" by having the dog sit and wait. Walk out to stand approximately six feet directly in front of the dog. With a piece of food in both hands, hold both hands up around your waist. Drop one hand only —

Start teaching "side" by having the dog sit and wait.

The dog should come to the hand that is dropped by your side.

it doesn't matter which one — and say "side" or "close" or whatever you choose to use for the command. The dog may require a release word like "okay" to come out of the wait.

The dog should come to the hand that is dropped by your side. Keep the other hand up by your waist. Click and treat. To get the click and treat, the dog should end up beside you, facing the same direction as you are. The goal is to teach the dog to run beside you, not in front of you. Many dogs try to cut off their handlers, but we want to teach them that the best place to be is beside us. To help the dog understand this, feed where you want him to be — beside you and with the hand closest to the dog.

Once the dog is succeeding on one side, repeat the steps on the other side using the other hand. The dog will quickly figure out the food is only available from the hand that is down by your side.

I recommend that you require a super high-drive dog to bring himself under control and sit when he is learning this exercise. As the dog begins to come in reliably, start to induce a sit, simply by lifting your hand up slightly. No verbal sit command is required, as most dogs will offer the sit if the food is lifted up and back slightly. I don't ask all dogs to do the sit, especially dogs that are tentative or less confident.

On course, I personally use a hand signal for the "side" command, although some people prefer a verbal only and use a different word for the right side and left side. I teach the exercise with a verbal "side" command but later I prefer to proof it using body language alone whenever possible. I want my dog to be able to see me across the field running away and know to come to the hand that is down by my side. Therefore it is important to remember not to allow your other hand to drop or flap when teaching this. It is beneficial to work with someone else to watch you and remind you about the other hand.

Once your dog is performing the "side" exercise reliably from a stationary position, add some movement. Drop your hand, give your command, and start walking forward. The second the dog catches up to you, click and stop moving, and give him the treat. Remember to feed the dog beside you, not in front. Then try it on the other side.

Your next step is to do it at a jog, then at a run.

Finally, try sending your dog to a curved tunnel, and as he comes out, run away, drop a hand with the treat in it, and see if he figures out to go to that dropped hand. Click and treat, and have a big play! This is a great exercise for less motivated dogs that are food driven. It can help them to drive out of tunnels faster.

Swing and Around

You can use these two commands to move your dog from one side to your other side. It comes in so handy in many situations. Here are a few:

- **Start line:** Use "swing" or "around" to line the dog up on the start line. How many times have you watched handlers moving all over the place to try to get the dog lined up? In the end they resort to physically placing the dog in the position. With the "swing" or "around" commands, the handler can stand still and the dog can line himself up with no messing around. It is neat, tidy and avoids adding pre-run stress to dog or handler.

- **Snooker:** Wouldn't you love to be able to move the dog from one side to the other at a full run when you are trying to get them in between equipment? Use the "swing" or "around" in snooker to help keep the dog focused on you and off the wrong equipment!

- **In place of a blind cross:** Use this at the end of contacts or weave poles to have the dog change sides. Rather than running in front of the dog doing a blind cross at the end of the contacts or poles, have the dog do the work and move to the other side of you while you continue running.

- **Line up for contact equipment:** I use "swing" or "around" to help my small dogs have a straight approach to the contact equipment after a tunnel. You can cue the dog verbally inside the tunnel to come around you as a post, lining them up for the contact obstacle.

When you teach swing and around think of an obedience finish.

When you teach swing and around think of an obedience finish. The only difference is that the dog will be able to do it in both directions. I use "around" for my dog to move from my right side to my left side, and "swing" to move the dog from my left to my right side.

Stage One: Lure Method

1. Start with your dog in front of you. Put food or toys in both hands.

2. Lure the dog around your right side with your right hand.

3. When the dog is behind your back, show him the food or toy in your left hand and bring him into a sit on your left side, facing the same way you are.

4. Use the lure three times only, and then try without the lure.

Alternate Stage One: Hand Target Method

1. If you have a good hand target, you can put out one hand beside you and slightly back and wait for the nose touch.

2. Drop the other hand beside and slightly behind you and have the dog continue around for the second touch and a cookie.

Stage Two: Name It

1. When you're able to drop the second lure or hand target, add the "around" command.

2. Gradually fade the signal until the dog can do it on a verbal command only.

Stage Three: Train the Other Side

1. Follow the steps in Stages One and Two, only start with the left hand, so the dog passes your left side and ends up on your right side.

2. Name this your "swing" side change.

Stage Four: Side to Side

1. Work until you have your dog doing both "swing" and "around" on a verbal cue, with no body cues or signals.

2. Now, start the dog at your side instead of in front of you. The dog should start in heel position on one side and move behind you to your other side.

Stage Five: Add Motion

1. Walk forward, pause and give your "swing" or "around" command, then walk forward again. Reinforce with food or a tug toy close to you.

2. Walk forward while you give the command to change sides.

3. Try it at a jog.

4. Have the dog do it at a full run.

5. Have the dog change sides in the middle of a full course of the dog's favourite equipment!

6. Once the dog can easily switch back and forth while you run through his favourite equipment without trying to take the equipment, start to release the dog to a piece of equipment now and then. Then use your "close" command to bring the dog back and switch sides again.

This helps the dog learn to transition from handler focus to obstacle focus and back to handler focus quickly and happily. Another end result of teaching these commands is that the dog learns that working in close and not taking equipment can be just as fun and reinforcing as taking equipment. This will eliminate the "my dog wants to work 15 feet away from me all the time" syndrome.

If you're working on this stage with a puppy, do a lot of playing close to you. Then randomize your work by sending him out to a toy and then ask him to stay close for a toy. You could also send out to a tunnel. The puppy will learn early in his training that going out to do the tunnel is fun but so

I say, "Ready" and they all freeze.

is coming in! Once you name swing and around, *never* use a hand signal for them. This will become confusing later when you are running with your dog. Always use a verbal cue *only*.

Front

I use the "front" command to help the dogs to drive in to me.

Teach front by rewarding the dog for coming directly in front of you and close enough to touch his head. I use the basic recall to reinforce the front position. Call the dog and offer a cookie right between your knees.

Once the dog understands where "front" is, start to spin as you say, "Front." This encourages the dogs to run to find your front. As long as I keep moving, the dog should keep trying to find the "front" position. When the dog finds front, face him, and click and tug. You can occasionally ask for a sit before you reward.

Next, add a tunnel to the exercise. Send the dog into the tunnel and when he comes out, tell him, "Front!" As he comes in, click and play. Then you can start to spin to make the dog try to get to your front. Keep it fun and play a lot.

Go!

I want the word "go" to initiate an immediate response of "run out ahead of me as fast as you can!" I start teaching this command by just using the word when I know the pup or dog will likely run. For example when I open the door to let everyone out in the yard they each get released with their name and a "Go!" They all run straight out to the yard one after the

Then I say, "Go!" in a sharp and intense voice. They all take off running away from me, chasing each other.

other. The chase drive helps associate the "Go!" with running fast.

I also use my toys to teach "go on." Hold the dog by the collar, throw the toy out in front and release them saying, "Go!" I also use the go command when I throw a Frisbee or anything my dog likes to chase. If I need to increase drive I will hold the dog that is learning the command, throw the Frisbee or toy for one of my experienced dogs and after the first dog takes off after the toy, I release the new dog with an encouraging, "Go!" They really start to drive out on the word.

When I take the dogs for a walk in a big open area, they all run around for the first little bit and then they come back for the "Go!" game. I say, "Ready" and they all freeze, then I say, "Go!" in a sharp and intense voice. They all take off running away from me, chasing each other. After they run a fair distance away, they circle back, then come and stand in front of me waiting to "go!" again. It is fun to watch them standing there, quivering and waiting for the word, then turning on a dime and bolting away as fast as they can. They love it and it is a game with purpose.

I am essentially doing backward restrained recalls using the other dogs as the lure. The drive to run away fast on the word "go!" becomes stronger and stronger because they have to work much harder to catch the other dogs than they do to catch me. Later, I use this drive I've created on obstacles with the dog chasing a toy.

Footwork for Crosses

Footwork has always been a big part of our competitive obedience training and when working with Wendy Pape, I realized we really need to pay more attention to what our feet tell our dogs in agility as well. I teach my dogs to cue off my feet for all of the work I do around or leading up to a jump. Sometimes I am amazed at how far away my dogs can read my feet!

Crosses are handling maneuvers you do on the course to help the dog to read which way they are going next. Our dogs are running through the course very quickly and we will never be faster than the dog (we hope!). So we need to have some effective communication with the dog that helps them know where we are going next. There are four basic types of crosses.

1. **Front Crosses:** This is when the handler crosses in front of the dog on the course while the dog is performing the previous piece of equipment. The handler never takes his eyes off his dog as he is rotating towards the dog. This cross relies on the handler's ability to send

the dog away to perform a piece of equipment on his own, which allows the handler time to get into position. Front crosses can speed up the course by allowing the handler to take shortcuts and tell the dog ahead of time where he is going next. The front cross is done on a curve and will result in the dog changing sides. If the dog starts on your right hand side, after the cross he should be on your left hand. Front crosses generally help the dog focus on the handler and shorten his stride. It tightens up a fast dog's turns. Front crosses allow slower, less confident dogs to keep up their speed because they know what is coming next.

2. **Rear Crosses:** These are when the handler crosses behind the dog while the dog is executing or approaching the next piece of equipment. Rear crosses are probably the most difficult of the crosses to do well. They require the handler to be able to send the dog ahead in order to cross behind. It is similar to waiting while you let someone else go through a door ahead of you. Again, the dog will start on your right and end on your left. Many people with fast dogs rely on rear crosses. The ability to do a great rear cross comes in handy but some courses are designed in such a way that a rear cross is just not going to allow the handler enough control of the dog in the next part of the course.

3. **Blind Crosses:** These are when the handler crosses in front of the dog with his back to the dog. This is a risky cross on jumps if the dog is very fast. However, if you have a knee problem it is easier on your knees than the front cross. Sometimes if you mix up blind and front crosses on the jump sequences the dog becomes confused about which arm to come to. I have seen this a lot when judging; you can see the indecision on the dogs' face when he is looking at his handlers' back. I prefer my students pick one or the other and be consistent. I do use blind crosses when the dog is in the tunnel and cannot see me as long as I can get to the new position before the dog comes out of the tunnel.

4. **Static Crosses:** These occur when the handler changes side while the dog is not moving, such as on the table or while the dog is holding a contact.

In this section, we'll also discuss footwork for a wrap. A wrap is not a cross. There is no change of side as the dog starts on the left hand and finishes on the left hand. However, it's a useful basic handling maneuver when the handler wants the dog to turn very tightly around the jump standard or wing.

I teach the front cross, rear cross and wrap on the flat before we do any equipment. Handlers should first learn the footwork without their dogs. It helps the handler understand and execute the footwork properly. Once they have it on the flat alone they can add in the dog. Once the handler and dog can do it on the flat we move to using just one jump. The footwork cues help the handler communicate with the dog quickly and effectively.

Front Cross Footwork

A front cross can be done on the take-off side or the landing side of a jump. It can also be a counter rotation. A counter rotation is when the dog does a 180-degree turn around the jump standard.

1. Start with the dog on your left side in a sit, facing the same way you are, and place a toy or target behind and between you.

2. Step back with the leg closest to the dog — in this case your left leg — and turn to face the toy. This first step back will eventually

Front Cross: Step back with the leg closes to the dog and turn to face the toy. The dog should turn towards you.

become the dog's cue that you want him to turn towards you and respond to the front cross.

3. Your body will open up to your dog which is a natural invitation for him to look at you. The dog should turn towards you.

4. Step through with your other foot — in this case the right foot — and point it at the toy as you tell your dog to "get it." The dog should end up on your right side.

5. When you and the dog can do steps 1 to 4 smoothly, repeat the steps with the dog starting on your right.

Rear Cross Footwork

1. Start with the dog on your left side in a sit, facing the same way you are.

2. Place the toy beside and slightly behind the dog's left side.

3. Using the foot closest to the dog — in this case your left foot — step in front of the dog. The dog should turn away from you, towards his left to where he knows the toy is waiting for him. When you step in front, try to be close enough to block the dog from turning in towards you. You can place the toy in such a spot that the dog can literally stare at the toy with his head away from you to start. Then put the toy farther around the dog so that the turn is more dramatic. Then wait for the dog to look back at you before you release to the toy. Eventually, this step in front of the dog should cue the dog to turn away from you.

Rear cross: Using the foot closest to the dog step in front of the dog.

The dog should turn away from you, towards his right to where he knows the toy is waiting for him.

4. When the dog completes the turn, step in behind the dog with your right foot and say "get it." The dog should finish on your right side.

5. When you and the dog can do steps 1 to 4 smoothly, repeat the steps with the dog starting on your right.

Footwork for a Wrap

1. Start with the dog on your left side in a sit, facing the same way you are.

2. Place the toy beside and slightly behind your right side.

3. Using the foot furthest from the dog this time — in this case your right foot — make a "T" with your right foot behind your left foot. This will bring your shoulder around and cause the dog to come around too. This step will become the dog's cue to wrap.

4. When the dog completes the turn, step forward towards the toy and say, "Get it." The dog should finish on your left side.

Up to now, we have done absolutely no equipment training. The previous exercises can take anywhere from six months to a year to train and perform well. If you start your puppy at 16 weeks on these skills, you will be

Wrap: Start with the dog on your left side in a sit, facing the same way you are.

Using the foot furthest from the dog this time – in this case your right foot – make a "T" with your right foot behind your left foot.

ready to start some pre-obstacle training right around 10 months to one year old, at which point you should get an X-ray of the puppy's shoulders, elbows and hips to ensure that all growth plates are closed.

Even an adult dog should have an X-ray of the hips, shoulders and elbows before he is ready to continue with training. Also, take a close look at the weight and physical condition of your dog to determine if agility should be in the dog's future. If physical issues limit your dog's future in agility, the flatwork skills you've taught him will lend themselves well to rally obedience or freestyle, sports which may be less strenuous on the dog's body.

If you have followed the progressions in previous chapters, by now your dog should be able to do the following behaviours that, in my opinion, should be performed proficiently before a dog is on any equipment.

- Sit-stay
- Down-stay
- Wait in the crate
- Front
- Back up
- Side/close
- Swing/around
- Hand target
- Drive in for a tug toy
- Retrieve a toy back to you
- 10 (plexiglass or lid) target touches in 12 to 15 seconds
- Wiffle-ball target from 15 feet away
- Go!
- Footwork for front cross
- Footwork for rear cross
- Footwork for wrap

Pre-obstacle Training

In the early days of my agility career there were not many ways to train the obstacles. Most people just did what they could to get the dogs over, in and onto the equipment. Today there are fabulously fun ways to help build confidence and develop much better obstacle performance skills. Breaking things down for the dogs allows them to learn at their own pace. The dogs that are not as confident are allowed to take their time when they are worried about something instead of being pushed to do the entire piece of equipment. Pre-obstacle exercises will help you to identify which obstacles your dog might have a problem with. If your dog does not like the wobble board then the teeter could be an issue. If your dog does not like going into the barrel, he may have problems with longer tunnels. If he doesn't like things touching his face, he may have some problems with weave poles or the chute fabric. This information will help you decide how long it may take and what approach you will use to train the full piece of equipment.

Once the dog can do all of the foundation skills from the previous chapters, we will start to add in some pre-obstacle training. Here are some exercises that will build the dog's confidence and make it easier to train the equipment later.

Teeter Totter

Wobble Boards

A wobble board is like a table top with a ball underneath. Wobble boards are a great way to get dogs used to movement under their feet. They learn to get on it and move it around, kind of like surfing. Some dogs love it, but it takes some dogs time and lots of reinforcement to overcome being nervous about standing on something that moves under their feet.

You can make your own wobble board by taking a four-foot by four-foot piece of plywood and putting a large tennis ball underneath. You will need to make a two-inch high by four-inch square box to hold the tennis ball in the centre. Paint and sand it like the contact equipment. I have a large one for big dogs and a three-foot by three-foot one for puppies.

1. Start by clicking and treating any interaction with the board. Initially, accept a nose touch, then a single foot on the board, then two feet on the side of the board that is resting on the ground.

2. Next, try to get the dog to put two feet on the raised side and make the board move. The idea is for the dog to lift both feet and slam the

When the dog has all four feet on the wobble board, place your reward so that he will make the board move.

board down. When he does, try to place your cookie reward so that the dog keeps his front feet on the board.

3. Work up to the dog getting three feet, then all four feet, on the board.

4. When the dog has all four feet on the board, place your reward so that the dog will make the board move as he gets the cookie. When the board moves, immediately click and treat and feed again in another spot that causes the dog to make the board move.

5. The next step is to only click if the dog has all four feet on the board and attempts to make it move on his own.

6. Once the dog will happily get on and roll the board around, start to deliver the treat off the board so that the dog has to turn around and run back onto the board to make it tip.

It may only take a couple of five-minute sessions to get the dog to this point, or it may take a couple of weeks. It all depends on the dog, his previous experience with moving surfaces in his environment, and the trainer's ability to let the dog learn at his own pace. Never force a worried dog to stay on the board. This will cause the dog to mistrust the handler and want to avoid the board altogether. If your dog is having problems or if you have been doing a low table with this dog and there is some confusion between the table and the wobble board, try this: put a small jump bump (a piece of PVC pipe about six-inches in diameter and cut in half) underneath each side so the wobble board only moves a small amount. Get the dog used to this. Then use a smaller bump on one side than on the other. Work up to only one bump and then remove the last bump. It is very important to allow a dog to progress at his own pace on this exercise. Never force the dog to get on or stay on the board.

Tippy Boards

A tippy board is a narrower version of the wobble board. It is a plank that has a piece of PVC pipe attached underneath it. Sometimes I leave the PVC unattached and let the board slide a bit.

I teach the tippy plank the exact same way I teach the wobble board. In the end, I want the dog to be

A tippy board is a narrower version of the wobble board.

able to run across the low and narrow board and have it move under his feet without the dog being worried. He should be able to run back and forth and stay on the plank. The board can also be used to teach the dog to approach it straight on rather than getting on sideways. Again, never make the dog stay on the board if he is uncomfortable or stressed.

Jumps

You can introduce your dog to the concept of jump standards and going over something early on in their training without having them actually jump anything. This is another way to build reinforcement into this obstacle without asking too much physically or mentally too soon.

Standards Alone

Start by getting the dog to run between two jump standards, or uprights. We use the wiffle ball to target the dog between the uprights.

Jump Bumps

Jump bumps are just pieces of PVC cut in half. We use PVC pipe in diameters of four inches, six inches and eight inches to create large or small bumps. Once the dog can run between the uprights, add a bump between them. Now the dog will learn to pay attention to that fact that there might

Left: We use the wiffle ball to target the dog between the uprights.

Once the dog can run between the uprights, add a bump between them.

be something under his feet. Keep the wiffle ball at the end to help the dog focus forward instead of focusing on the bump.

Start with one jump, and work up to two, three, four and five sets of jump standards with bumps. The dog should be running through the standards, away from the handler, to the wiffle ball. The handler does not run with the dog.

The jump standards and bumps should be placed close enough together that the dog bounces through them — meaning that he does not walk or take extra strides between each bump. For puppies, the bumps will be two to three feet apart, depending on the size of the puppy, and for adult dogs, the bumps should be three to four feet apart, depending on the size of the dog. If the dog is adding steps in between, bring the bumps closer together, and if he is taking two at a time, move them farther apart.

It doesn't matter if the dog touches the wiffle ball and turns to run back over the jumps. At this point we just want the dog to experiment with the equal spacing between the jump standards and bumps.

Table

Train the table and the wobble board at the same time as you may find your table breaks down a bit when you introduce your dog to the wobble board. The dog should be able to lie down, sit and stand on a verbal command alone before he starts any table work.

Start all dogs with a 10-inch table. Practice having the dog get on the table and do sits, downs and stands. You want the dog to learn to get on the table and do something. You never want the dog to get on the table, then stand and stare at you as so many competition dogs do. Start by teaching an automatic sit, as it gets the dog to drop his rear immediately. The sit provides the foundation for the down on the table as it prevents the "butt in the air" syndrome — a sort of play bow — that so many dogs offer on the table. The rest of the steps in training a table are covered on page 120.

Plank

I like to have the dogs work on a solid plank at the same time as they are doing wobble board and tippy board work so they don't assume the board will always move under them.

You can make a plank by painting a 12-inch wide by six-foot board with exterior paint and sprinkled with silica sand.

Stage One: Plank familiarization

1. Start by setting the plank on the ground and letting the dog offer different behaviours on it. Reward the dog for nose touches, jumping over it, walking on it, and eventually running along the plank. Use the same principles as with tippy board training. Never force a dog to stay on the plank if he doesn't want to. Ideally we want the dog to get on the plank and go to the end and stand still until he is released off the board for a toy. If you are going to be doing two-on two-off contacts, shape the dog to stand on the end with all four feet on the board. We want the dog to try different things. Eventually only standing still will be reinforced. Work on your release cue at the same time.

2. Do step one with both slatted and slatless planks.

Stage Two: Elevated plank

1. Once the dog is happy walking on the plank on the floor, rest the ends of the plank on two low tables. I use the 10-inch legs at first. Get the dog to walk the plank from table to table. Start by walking with the dog, and click and treat along the board for any movement forward. I start by rewarding movement with his front feet.

Shape the dog to move along both slatted and slatless planks.

2. Begin to click and reward the dog for forward motion with his back feet only. Rear end movement propels the dog forward faster.

3. Progress to the point where the dog will go across the plank in one fluid motion. Click and feed at the end of the board and on each table.

4. Work to get the dog more confident on the plank and start to have him actually run along the board. Try to stay in the centre of the board, between the two tables, facing the dog, so he isn't picking up any cues to run from you. Try to get the dog to initiate the crossing to the other table all on his own. Click for speed and confidence and throw the cookies onto the table ahead of the dog.

Also teach the dog how to jump up and turn around on the board. Many dogs don't know where their back feet are on a plank and will only turn one way. Try to get them comfortable both ways. Allow them to get off of it if they want. Only reward on the board.

You can also elevate the plank on one end only. Work on having the dog stand on the end without his rear end falling off the side. He should hold his position until he is released.

Once the dog is happy walking on the plank on the floor, rest the ends of the plank on two low tables.

Weave Poles

Shaping Poles

I start my puppies on the weave pole chute with wires opened right up so that they are not even touching the poles. I work on speed and entrances, letting them find their own way into the channel from different angles and speed. I make sure it stays fun; to the dog, it's just a game we play with the toy.

As I am letting the puppies or new dogs experiment with these channels we are also shaping interaction with sets of two and three poles in other sessions. I do not work channels and two or three poles all in the same day.

I use two and three weave poles to get the dogs accustomed to something bumping their shoulders, and to help the dogs understand that the poles don't move, but that they have to move through them. I use only two or three poles because I do not want puppies or green dogs doing any repetitive bending of the spine until they are mature or have the appropriate health clearance.

Start by clicking and treating any interaction with the poles. It can be something as simple as a nose going past a pole, although be careful not to click this too many times or you get the dog targeting the poles.

Click for behaviours such as walking between any of the poles and stepping on the base of the poles. Don't worry about "weaving" or entrances initially. You just want the dog to move in and around the poles on his own.

I start my puppies on the weave pole chute with wires opened right up.

Try to place the reinforcer in between the poles or out at the end of the poles to keep his head moving out of the poles straight.

Do not reward a frantic dog that knocks over the poles or crashes into them with his shoulders. Tape or stake the poles down and only reward if the poles do not get rocked back and forth. Obviously some movement will be necessary but allowing a dog to crash into them continuously will only encourage poor and unsafe poles later, possibly ending the dog's career early if he continues to slam into weave poles with his shoulders.

The Chute

The best way to do this method of training weave poles is five days a week for five to 10 minutes at a time. Therefore, to do it properly, you will need to have a set of chute poles and wires at home. It will take about three to four months to train a highly motivated dog. A less-motivated dog will need more time and will require more effort on the part of the trainer to learn when the dog is motivated to work and what motivates him to run fast. Never do weave pole training when the dog is not interested in working. Wait until the dog is highly motivated to work for you. Try training when you first get home from work or before dinner.

Week One:

1. **Walk the dog through the chute on leash.**

   Make sure the chute is wide enough for dog and handler to get through together. Two feet or so is usually fine. Click and treat in the chute, especially if the dog is nervous. Do this until the dog is comfortable with the wires and poles beside him.

   Vary the click so that sometimes it is at the beginning, the middle or the end. Try to time your click so that the dog's head is low and forward when you click, not up and looking at you like obedience heeling. We want the dog's head down and focused forward in the weave poles.

   Always treat or play after you click. Do this exercise until the dog is pulling you through the poles and is not worried at all about the poles or wires. You can go from clicking in the poles to clicking and throwing a toy at the end of the poles.

2. **Call the dog through the chute to you.**

   Place the dog in the entrance of the chute. You may need to start with the dog partway into the poles. Some dogs should even start halfway through the chute. Walk through the chute to the end and call the dog through. Praise and play. You are looking for confidence, speed and enthusiasm coming through the chute. Back the dog up gradually so that he is waiting outside the chute entrance and running through on his own. Work this with the dog lined up straight to the chute opening until the dog can be back at least 10 feet from the chute and do a recall through it.

Weeks Two and Three:

3. Challenge the dog to find the entry.

Set the dog at odd angles to the poles. Gradually make it more difficult. The dog will be learning to find the entrance to the poles so do not skip this step. You are still calling the dog through to you. This step takes about two weeks to get the dog to actually understand that it is his job to find the opening regardless of where he is started.

If the dog makes a mistake, the wires will correct him, so the handler should *not* correct. If the dog is unable to find the entrance to the poles, go back to the straight-on approach until the dog is successful again. If the dog pops out of the poles, never put the dog back in the poles from the middle (where he popped out) either in practice or competition. The poles are one obstacle to be done from beginning to end. You will confuse the dog by allowing him to go in and out in the middle.

You can narrow the chute down to a little wider than the dog's body width as you do this step. Each time you narrow the chute, set the dog in a straight line with the poles or even in the entrance for the first few times. The dog should not have to bend his body yet.

Every time you make it harder to do one thing, make something else easier. For instance, if you make the chute more narrow, set the dog up for a straighter approach to the chute. You want the dog to be able to race through those poles.

Weeks Four and Five:

4. Send the dog through to a toy.

Place the dog in a wait at the end in a straight line with the poles. Place a toy, wiffle ball or a closed food target at the other end. Return and stand parallel to the dog and send him through to the toy. Click and play when he exits the poles. Run out to the side and meet the dog to play and praise so that the dog does not run back through the poles to meet you. Initially, keep the toy in line with the poles. Then start to let the toy be a bit off centre. The dog needs to understand to run through the poles no matter what.

When sending the dog, concentrate on not showing the dog any forward motion. You want the dog to go on his release word alone. If the dog won't go to the toy on his own, have a helper entice the dog. Try not to have the handler in the picture other than to give the release word and to reward for success.

This step is the one to spend the most time on; you are looking for speed and enthusiasm. Spend a good couple of weeks making this the best game ever!

Remember the dog is still not actually weaving so do not name this "weave" at this point, especially if you are getting inconsistent responses from the dog on this piece of equipment. Never name something that is half-trained and not perfect.

Weeks Six and Seven:
5. Challenge the dog to find the entry – again.

Begin to have the dog sit off centre from the poles again and gradually work up to more angled approaches. The dog will be running out to the toy and he should know this game very well before you add angled approaches.

If the dog looks completely confused the first time you do this, then simply help him by making the angles less difficult. Don't be in a hurry. This is a very important step for the dog. Again, take about two weeks to work angles and record how your dog is doing. Do not narrow the chute.

6. Change position.

Always do each exercise from the right side and left side of the dog as well as behind the dog and off to the side about six feet from the poles. When calling the dog through, stay in line with the poles in the beginning. This will help the dog learn that poles are something he does by himself. We will add ourselves into the picture later.

Weeks Eight:
7. Add a tunnel to the end of the poles.

Send through the poles to the tunnel or any obstacle he likes and does well. I don't like to use jumps as there are too many chances for the dog to knock bars or go under the jump. I would prefer to use a tunnel, table or tire to send to. Of course your dog must be able to "go" to these obstacles from at least 15 feet away as you will be sending him down the chute and on to the next obstacle instead of running with the dog. As you throw the toy, make sure you get it out before the dog has a chance to look back at you. Try sending to the toy when it is off-set on the ground so that he learns to focus on the obstacles first and then get the toy.

If you are working alone, put the toy in an ice cream bucket so the dog can't get it if he makes an error. You can run out after the dog has completed the exercise correctly and open the bucket. Make a big deal of opening the bucket. Dogs love it when you make a fool of yourself!

Week 9:

8. Challenge the dog to find the entry – yet again.

With another obstacle after the poles, add in the gradual off-angle entries to the poles. Vary your position without running with the dog. Try working with a tunnel at the beginning of the poles. This forces the dog to have to cut in to find the entry to the poles.

Week 10:

9. Do more difficult entries to the poles.

Here you will find out if your dog truly understands where the poles start and how to find them. When working entries, use your body to move the dog around a bit. Always be at least six feet from the poles when sending the dog in and do not run beside the poles with the dog. Remain at the beginning of the poles and reward the dog out at the end of the poles (or the obstacle after the poles) with the toy or wiffle ball to keep the dog driving forward. Make sure you step to the side to prevent the dog from back-weaving the poles.

10. Start to proof the dog.

Place the toy along side the poles about half way down and see if the dog can weave past the toy. Then place the toy on the base of the poles and see if the dog can weave over the toy. Roll the toy past the

---

Keep your Rate of Reinforcement High

If my dog "fails" to negotiate a training sequence or respond to a command more than twice in a row, it is likely a handler error: my cue is not clear or I am asking too much. I need to remember to reward my dog for something easier or for simply trying. If the reinforcement rate drops too low, my dog will likely quit and find something or someone else more reinforcing. If my dog genuinely tries to do what I ask and misreads my body, or I miscue the dog, the dog still needs to be rewarded. I can do this by tugging and playing with the dog. If I don't want the dog to repeat the last mistake, I can ask him to come to me and do something simple, such as a sit or a down or a trick, so I can reward.

dog when he is in the poles. Throw the toy across the line of poles in front of him as he is weaving. Also, start adding in some movement from the handler. Start to run down the poles alongside the dog. Run past the poles and get him to chase you for the toy.

Week 11:

11. Start to close the chute.

Gradually move the poles closer, about one inch at a time. Repeat all steps from 2 to 10 with the chute at this new width. You will probably find that the progression will go faster. Always work for enthusiasm and accuracy at each step.

As the poles get closer you will lose some speed until the dog is comfortable again. If he is normally a fast dog and is slowing down, don't worry about it, just encourage him to work through his tentativeness. If you have been doing your two- and three-pole work at the same time he will not be worried about the poles getting closer. He will pick up again when he is sure of what you want. Sometimes you have to sacrifice speed for accuracy for a while.

> **Try Again**
>
> If you send the dog to the weave poles and he spins, barks, hesitates or head checks before he goes, bring him back and move a bit closer. Try again. He needs to go to the poles on one command in one motion. Do not reinforce any spinning, barking or hesitation.

Do not close the poles to the point that the dog has to bend his spine until the dog is at least one year old and all the growth plates have closed.

12. Remove the wires and name it.

Once you have worked up to the point that the poles are completely together and you have done all steps 2 to 8 again, you can start to remove the wires. This is the time to name the poles if you are happy with the way your dog is performing them. Remember, you get what you name, just like you get what you click!

I like to just pull the wires up to the top of the poles, starting with the centre wires. I work the poles with all the wires on for about two months. I start to add other obstacles and put the poles in a sequence. Work on speed into the poles (using lots of jumps and spread jumps before them) as well as off-angle entries. Try distractions that might cause the dog to make mistakes, such as tunnels after the poles, tunnels beside the poles, and toys on the ground beside the poles.

Then I start to remove the middle wires. I leave the entrance and exit wires on for a long time. Work all steps from 2 to 8 including the proofing exercises with the one wire missing or pushed up. Then try two wires and so on. Use your judgement to decide how many wires your dog can handle being removed. Vary which ones are off. Progress only if the dog is understanding the excercise.

If you get more than two mistakes in a row, place the wires back on or push them down a bit. You do not want too many repetitions of the dog popping out halfway through. However, a couple of errors while the dog is figuring it out is not a bad thing. He needs to have a choice about what he will do, and learn that only the right choice will earn a reward.

If the dog completely falls apart, re-evaluate the process. Did you rush through any of the foundation work? Be honest and fair instead of making your dog take the brunt of your frustration when he gets confused. Don't be afraid to go back to an easier step.

Once I start my weave pole training and I am on a straight line of poles, I will come back to the two and three-pole work and work on entrances, but I never do this with a dog under one year old. The twos and the threes are great for refining problems in the understanding of the poles. Is it entries, exits, or completing all poles that needs refining? Once the dog is proficient on all of those things individually, then you can work to chain them together.

For example, a dog that has problems with entries does not need to try to do the entry and finish 12 poles. This is muddling up your criteria for the dog. Keep the criteria in weave-pole training clear in your mind. Work on twos or threes until he has full understanding of pole entries.

If your dog needs help completing all the poles, try putting out sets of poles with six-foot spaces in between. Put out a set of two, then a set of three, then a set of four, then a set of six, then a set of 12 in a line. Can the dog consistently complete all the poles in the line? A dog that understands to weave all the poles he sees will not have a problem continuing down the line.

Then try putting 18 poles out in a line, then 24, then 48 and so on. The first time I entered Bryn in the 60 weave pole challenge she had never done more than 12 poles in a line in her life. She did the 60 poles perfectly three times and was the only dog to make her entry correctly the first time every time. The first time I put Feyd through 60 poles I had injured my calf muscle and couldn't walk, so I recalled him through the 60 poles. He did them perfectly! These dogs obviously understand weave poles.

My last two puppies have learned their weave poles on Susan Garrett's 2x2 method. I had been a die-hard chute trainer and it has worked great for me but Susan once said to me, "Try the 2x2 method and if you don't like it you can always go back to what worked before." She was right and I love the 2x2 method. For more information on 2x2 weave pole training see Susan Garrett's book *Shaping Success* or *DogSport* magazine issue March/April 2004 and May/June 2004.

Single Obstacle Training

Once you start to actually do equipment, it is very easy to get caught up in doing more and more pieces. People tend to want to "get going" so that they can get their dogs running full courses. I understand that this is an exciting part of the training, but your dog will need time to learn and build confidence on each piece of equipment. Then the dog needs time to increase the speed at which he can do each. Then you need to do some distraction work for each piece.

Photograph by Len Silvester

General Principles for Obstacle Training

As my training progresses and gets more difficult, I try to remember that it shouldn't be about training the equipment. It should be about finding and creating opportunities to reward and play with your dog. If you think about how to set the dog up to get things right and provide as many opportunities for him to play and be rewarded, you will likely never go wrong and your dog will learn to love agility!

Here are some general principles to keep in mind as you train the equipment:

1. **Train the behaviour (piece of equipment) accurately.**

   Decide exactly how you want that piece of equipment performed. Do you want a two-on, two-off contact or a running contact? Do you want a tire performance in which the dog does not touch the tire or will you allow the dog to bank off the tire? Do you want the dog to get on the table and immediately do a down position or will you accept having to give a second command for the down?

2. **Increase the speed at which the dog can perform the behaviour.**

   By going to a variable rate of reinforcement, you will increase the speed at which the dog will perform the behaviours. You can choose to reward a slow down on the table with light praise instead of a cookie. You can throw the toy only when the dog runs through the tunnel as opposed to walking or trotting through.

3. **Add distractions to the behaviour.**

   Have the handler move a bit, place a toy on the ground, put another piece of equipment out, or have another dog tugging on the sidelines. Increase distractions only to the level the dog can handle. For more ideas, read about proofing in Chapter 9.

4. **Change the location of the behaviour.**

   Dogs need to be able to perform the equipment in various locations and environments. Go to another training facility, go to fun matches, train in a friend's backyard, or lug some equipment to a park. Try any place that is safe.

Try to remember to follow these principles in order. You'll run into problems if you don't. For instance, adding distractions to a dog that does not understand how to do the behaviour accurately will lead to confusion and

What's in a Name?

When you train each obstacle, think carefully about what you are going to call the equipment when it is time to name it. Words like "tunnel," "table," "tire," and "teeter" sound much too similar for the dogs to ever learn to discriminate. I use "through" for the tunnel, "bench" for the table, "seesaw" for the teeter and "leap" for the tire. Other options for these obstacles I have heard are "box" for the table, "hoop" or "ring" for the tire, "tip" or "bang" for the teeter and "under" for the tunnel. Choose names that make sense to you and that do not sound too similar to other obstacles.

frustration. The dog will not have the opportunity to be reinforced. A low rate of reinforcement due to too many errors can cause stress-related problems. See page 29 for more information on signs of stress during training.

The distractions stage is an extremely important one that tends to get missed. It will teach your dog to work under all types of pressure situations. It is unlikely you will be able to mimic the trial situation at home. It is very difficult for handlers to conjure up the scent of the stress and nerves we feel going into a ring. Therefore, we must proof other types of stress for the dog, which will enable him deal with our ring stress more easily and keep his mind on his job.

Train the Physical Behaviour First

I try to shape the physical behaviour for each obstacle before I put a name on it. I need to see how the dog feels about each piece of equipment before I add a cue. If there are going to be issues for the dog with the movement, height, looks, or sound of a particular obstacle, I want to know that. Then I will do my best to give the dog time to become desensitized to those things before I continue with that obstacle. I will try to address each "issue" by breaking it down and doing some more pre-obstacle work on that problem.

Some common equipment problems I see are teeter movement and sound, dogwalk and A-frame height, tunnel colour, table texture (especially for smooth-coated dogs like Whippets and JRT's), jump bars that fall, jump standards that get knocked over, tire movement, and the feeling of chute fabric on a dog's head. As I start training each piece of equipment I will just let the dog interact with the obstacle and see what bothers him and what doesn't. This will tell me how best to approach the training and tell me if I need to do some desensitizing on certain characteristics of the equipment.

Initial Verbal and Physical Cues

I never want to name a behaviour that is incomplete or that has problems. For example, if I try to put a new dog on a full-height teeter without any pre-obstacle teeter work and I name it "teeter" and the dog spooks and falls off, I have now named the scary obstacle "teeter." If I continue to train it using that word I may wind up with permanent avoidance of the teeter. Instead, when I'm training an obstacle, I try to use a simple body cue that indicates I want the dog to go to the obstacle in front of me.

My body cue tells my dog to go to what I am facing. It starts with a neutral position. I face perpendicular to the obstacle with the dog facing me. When I have the dog's attention I say, "Okay" or "Go" and turn 90 degrees to face the obstacle I am working on. This gives the dog some body motion to help him move forward, but doesn't have the handler traveling towards the obstacle. The word releases the dog from focusing on me without me having to name the obstacle.

When the dog shows me a good solid understanding of the behaviour I want on that obstacle, I will begin to name it. When I add the verbal cue for the obstacle really depends on the dog. If I am getting the type of performance I want from the dog on the piece of equipment, I will add the word. Initially I say the verbal cue and support it with the body cue that I have been using. I will gradually drop the body cue and try to get the dog to go on the verbal cue alone.

I face perpendicular to the obstacle with the dog facing me.

Independent Performance

I train each piece of equipment individually with no other equipment around. Each piece needs to be trained from the following handler positions:

- Right side

- Left side

- Five feet back

- 10 feet back

- 20 feet back

- A 45-degree angle both right and left side

- A 90-degree angle both right and left side

- Bi-directionally (with the exception of the teeter and chute)

Directional Commands

If the piece of equipment needs to have directional commands applied to it then I will add this to my list of behaviours to teach my dog on that piece of equipment. For example, if I am going to teach a left and right on a jump I will do that as part of my jump training. I may also want to teach a left and right out of a tunnel and also on the tire.

When I have the dog's attention I say, "Okay" or "Go" and turn 90 degrees to face the obstacle I am working on.

One obstacle may have many verbal cues, especially if you are training for directional commands as well. For example, a jump may have four different cues. One to turn right after the jump, one to turn left after the jump, one to come to the handler after the jump and one to continue on in a straight line before and after the jump. However, the command for the jump is still the same. For my dogs, a jump is "hup." So the verbal jump commands are: "hup right," "hup left," "hup front," and "go hup."

I believe each piece of equipment should be trained on a verbal cue alone and on a physical cue alone. Using both together will help enhance the behaviour and build confidence in a confusing situation such as a discrimination challenge at speed.

Single Obstacles

Obstacles are just like targets. I teach my dogs that if I am facing it, you should do something with it. You never want the dog to ignore an obstacle you are facing — especially when he is just starting his training.

Anticipation doesn't bother me. If I am walking past a table, tire, or jump on my way to the tunnel and my dog takes an obstacle, so be it — I faced it. I would never reward it, but I am not going to nag the dog about it either. If I don't want my dogs taking equipment then I will put them on leash or put the other equipment away, or walk around the other equipment so that it is not as tempting. At this point in their training, I want the dog to love the equipment and interact with it to get the toy.

The first four obstacles I train are the jump, tunnel, tire and table. These are the only obstacles we do in our "Agility Prep" class and our "Obstacle Performance 1 and 2" classes. Each class focuses on a different element of these four obstacles.

In Agility Prep we cover the initial teaching of these pieces of equipment. If the dogs are going to have any problems with jumping we will be able to see that in the obstacle training. The table also tells us a lot about the dog's physical abilities as dogs that have any kind of physical issues will likely not want to continually get up and lie down on the table. We will often see dogs that are dysplastic show signs of the problem during the jump and table training.

In Obstacle Performance 1 we start to add angles, distance and footwork to the obstacles. In Obstacle Performance 2 we start to sequence these four obstacles and introduce some handling. In this chapter, we will discuss how to train these pieces of equipment. Remember that we spend a lot of time working on only one piece of equipment. There will not be any other equipment around to distract or confuse the dog.

Jump Training

Here are the tools we use for our jump training:

- Clicker

- Toy that can be thrown that doesn't bounce

- Food

- Wiffle ball

- Jump bump

- One jump – wingless to start

Jump training is something that is far more complicated than we first thought. Of all the obstacles in agility I think the jumps are trained the least often and the least effectively. People believe because dogs naturally jump up, onto, and over things that they just know how to jump. Jumping, or jumping well, is in fact a long and complicated process that is just recently being addressed more and more in this sport. Many national championships have been won or lost over one jump bar.

Most of the dogs I see in competition really have no idea how to jump effectively or efficiently. Some are even what I would consider unsafe. My red border collie Sierra is one that can be considered unsafe when she is jumping at times. She has needed huge amounts of jump education and continually needs to be in at least one jump class per week or she will lose her technique very quickly. Her enthusiasm overrides her common sense at times and she will throw herself over jumps, not paying any attention to how she gets over them. This leads to slipping on the landings, crashing bars, hitting jump standards and landing in the middle of double jumps. Not a very pretty picture!

In my quest to find out more about jump training I attended Susan Salo's jump clinic in 2003. If I was looking for information on jump training I certainly found it! We now have a class dedicated solely to jumping. Dogs take a jump class once a week for the rest of their agility careers. We work on any number of jumping skills including patterns, grid work, bend work, scope work, distractions, send outs, footwork, diagonal jumping, and lots of one-jump work. This is a long and complicated process and will take up more space than I have in this book. I will instead focus on the one-jump work. Ideally, one-jump work should be done in conjunction with formal grid work.

From Bump to Bar

After your pre-obstacle training with the jump standards and jump bumps, start to introduce a low jump bar if the dog is physically capable of jumping. My definition of "physically capable" is that the growth plates are closed and the dog is free from any discomfort due to arthritis or other chronic joint injuries.

Once the dog will go out over the jump bump all on his own, either to a wiffle ball or just on a physical cue, you can start to train the jump bar the same way. Usually this goes very quickly as the pre-obstacle work has given the dog the general idea of what a jump is.

Place a wiffle ball or a toy on the ground for the dog to get after he completes the jump to keep his focus forward.

Jump Grid Work

Basic grid work consists of five jumps in a straight line spaced anywhere from three feet to six feet apart depending on the size of the dog. The first step in this process will be to get the dog to go over five low jumps in a row without the handler. The dog should "bounce" between jumps, which means he will not add any strides.

Start with one jump and work at a low height until the dog will go immediately over the jump on his own. Once I know there are no physical signs of discomfort when the dog is taking the jump, I will start to add in a second, third, fourth and finally a fifth jump in the line, the same as the jump-bump line. I keep the jumps very low — six inches for young and small dogs and 10 inches for mature and larger dogs.

You can back-chain this by doing one jump to the wiffle ball, then add a jump before the first jump, then add a jump in front of that one until you are at five jumps. This will not happen overnight and the goal is to get the dog to go over all the jumps without any forward motion from the handler. The dog must be able to hold a sit-stay and should go when he is released.

Keep the placement of your reinforcement in mind. Try to make sure that the dog is looking over the jump and not back at the handler when he jumps. Head position is very important in jumping and you do not want the head up and twisted back as the dog jumps. Place a wiffle ball or a toy on the ground for the dog to get after he completes the jump to keep his focus forward. Placement of the reward can positively or negatively affect the behaviour. Make sure you are either throwing the toy out ahead of the dog after he has made the commitment to jump and early enough to keep him moving forward, or place the toy out as a lure before the dog jumps.

Once the dog will go over the five jumps away from you then you are ready to start a jump class!

One Jump – Independant Performance

Work on one jump, gradually moving back from the jump. When I get the dog going out to the jump at least six feet on a body cue alone, I will add the "jump" command. You can use any command that makes sense to you. "Jump," "hup," and "over" are all common commands.

When the dog will go out to the jump in a straight line from six feet away on a verbal command and a small body turn, start to move further back. I would like a minimum of 10 feet to the jump, and more if I can get it.

Once I have a 10-foot send I will move back in closer to the six-foot mark and work on an angled approach to the jump. Concentrate on using the foot and arm and shoulder closest to the dog as you cue the dog to jump. You and the dog need to be on the same line, with your shoulders parallel to the dog's path over the jump.

Work at the six foot mark on both the right and left sides and continue to build distance from the jump. Make sure your placement of the reinforcement is appropriate for head and body position for jumping. Work until you get a nice 10-foot send from an angle on the jump from the right and the left side. Reward the dog on the far side of the jump. You are trying to reward the dog for going away from you so make sure the dog gets his reward away from you.

Once I have a nice 10-foot send straight to the jump, and from the right and the left sides of the jump, I work on my footwork over one jump. The front, rear and wrap foot work is described in the "Flatwork" section on page 84. Make sure you work with a good instructor! Work on a front cross on both sides, the rear cross on both sides and the wrap or post turns on both sides.

I also do diagonal jumping on one jump. Place the dog quite close to the jump and next to the wing of the jump with the bar set fairly low. Stand on the opposite side directly in front of him so you can draw a straight line over the jump between the two of you. Ask the dog to jump towards you on the diagonal from both a sit and a down position. The dog should not have room to take a stride into the jump. He should have to collect and hop over the bar.

Many dogs have a problem following through with their back feet and often land on the bar during this skill. If this happens, give the dog a bit more landing space but do not increase the take-off space. Let him work it out for

Work until you get a nice 10-foot send from an angle on the jump from the right and the left side.

himself. Dogs really do not like to land on or hit bars. They are honest and practical creatures who will try to make it more comfortable for themselves by not hitting the bar. Allow them to work this out on their own.

Work until the dog can jump diagonally at full height. I have found many dogs have a "good side" and a "bad side." Jumping from left to right may not be as easy as jumping right to left. Make a note in your training journal about which side is worse and make sure you work on it more. Also make a note of which back leg is on the outside of the jump on the bad side, this leg may need more strengthening or have an injury you need to keep an eye on.

When the dog is successful jumping diagonally towards you on both sides, begin to ask the dog to jump diagonally away from you. Stand directly beside the wing of the jump. Put the dog on your right or left side. Place a toy or target on the opposite side of the jump. Send the dog diagonally over the jump away from you. Practice this until you can send the dog from either side of the jump – and from either side of you – without the target or toy.

Place the dog quite close to the jump and next to the wing of the jump with the bar set fairly low.

Ask the dog to jump towards you on the diagonal from both a sit and a down position.

Figure 8

The next progression is to turn your diagonal jumping into a Figure 8. The goal is to be able to send the dog over the jump diagonally away from you and bring him around again to jump diagonally toward you, then once again around the jump standard. I use my verbal cue for "swing" and "around" as well as "hup left" and "hup right." I don't use any body language because it is not a handling maneuver and I don't want to confuse the dog with conflicting signals.

Tuck Jump

Place the dog quite close to the jump and directly in line with it with the bar set fairly low. Stand on the opposite side directly in front of him so you can draw a straight line over the jump between the two of you. Ask the dog to jump towards you on a straight line from both a sit and a down position. The dog should not have room to take a stride into the jump. He should have to collect and hop over the bar. Allow just enough space between you and the jump bar for the dog to tuck his rear under him and sit in front of you. If the dog hits the bar, move back a bit and give him a bit more room. You want the dog to have to pull his rear end underneath him to avoid hitting the bar. Work until the dog can do this at his full height. You may have to give him a bit more room for take-off at full height.

During one-jump training, the dogs should be working on their grid work including straight line and bended grids. We also use other jumping exercises we have developed over the years here at Pawsitive Steps. But that is for another book!

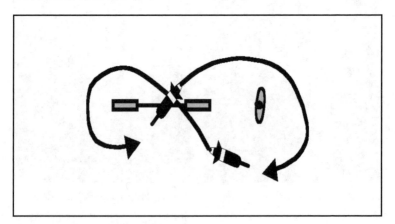

Turn your diagonal jumping into a figure 8.

Tire Training

When you train the tire, you'll need the same training tools as you used for training a jump:

- Clicker

- Toy that can be thrown but doesn't bounce

- Food

- Wiffle ball

When I start training the tire I just use a clicker and a hungry dog. I like to use food initially for the tire even with the not-so-food-motivated dogs as I find those are the ones that will likely blast through the tire and knock it over. I let the dog experiment with which space gets the cookie. Dogs will naturally try to go through the most convenient and efficient space. If that happens to be the side of the tire (between the bungee and the frame), then that is what they will try.

I only click and treat if the dog goes through the middle space. It does not take a clicker-savvy dog long to figure it out. At first, I will click and treat for going away through the tire and coming back through the tire. At some point, the dog will likely hit the tire and notice that it has a slingshot effect. Sometimes it will actually hit the dog and can startle him. If this happens, depending on the dog, simply ask for any easy behaviour and immediately reinforce the dog and then play if you can. If the dog is very afraid, simply don't react. Just reach out to stop the tire from wobbling.

Tuck jump: Place the dog quite close to the jump and directly in line with it with the bar set fairly low.

Ask the dog to jump towards you on a straight line from both a sit and a down position.

Walk away, do one of the "keep trying" exercises and get right back to work as if nothing happened. The worst thing you can do is reinforce the dog's fears.

You can also use your wiffle ball target to get the dog to focus on the centre of the tire and not around the edges. It seems to help nervous dogs concentrate on the wiffle ball instead of obsessing about the obstacle. Fade the wiffle ball as soon as possible by moving it farther and farther back. When the dog is driving through the tire, begin to click before the dog touches the wiffle ball and reinforce on the ground in front of the dog.

You can have someone else do the feeding at the wiffle ball if necessary. However, only do this three times and then get the person out of the picture, otherwise the second person becomes a huge cue to the dog instead of the tire.

Table Training

The dog must be able to do a "down" on a verbal command alone before he starts this exercise. Start all dogs on a 10-inch table.

Start by choosing a table command — "bench," "box," and "table" are all possibilities. You'll also need a release word, which you may have already trained. Some possible release words are, "okay," "all done," "let's go," and "break." You'll always use your release word to take the dog off the table.

The goal of using this method of training is that you'll never have to resort to asking your dog for the "down" once you have said "table." If you

At first, the dog only needs to get on the table to earn a reward.

Once he is driving to the table and jumping up, add the sit.

absolutely have to second-command the dog, it should be the "table" command only.

1. With the dog on leash, start about 10 feet away and run towards the table. Say your table command before the dog gets to it (approx six feet before). When the dogs jumps on the table, click and treat (C&T).

    Say "okay" and take him away from the table. The dog only needs to get on the table; there is no other requirement at this point. You are looking for the dog to look ahead to the table and initiate getting onto it before you get there. Click front feet on, reward and release. Then C&T back feet on and release. Finally, C&T when the dog turns around to look at you.

    At first, stand close enough to feed the dog. After several repetitions, start to hang back a bit and see if the dog will stay on the table and wait for you to come in to feed him.

2. Once the dog is happily going out and jumping on the table, ask the dog to sit once he is up on the table, then C&T. Say, "okay" and release the dog off the table. Do this at least five times with a verbal "sit" command alone. You want to see the dog anticipating the sit.

3. This time, when you say, "table" and run toward it, do not ask for the sit; see what the dog offers you. Most likely the dog will sit, as that is what is most recent in his mind. If he sits on his own, C&T. Do this at least five times with a click and treat each time he sits and always release with your release command. Try to make sure you are not moving on your release command.

When the dog is offering an automatic sit, add the down.

4. Start this stage when the dog is going out and automatically sitting when he gets on the table. Run towards the table, say "table," wait for the sit, and ask for a down. C&T the down, release. Do this five or six times with only a verbal "down" command. The dog should start to anticipate the down.

5. Run to the table and give your "table" command. Then don't say a

word and wait the dog out. Likely he will sit, and then if he doesn't get the click for that, he will try something else; he will most likely offer a "down" next. When he offers the down, C&T. Release.

From now on you will only click and treat an automatic down. Never verbally ask for the down; just wait the dog out. We are teaching the dog that the only way to get the treat is to do an automatic down. The dog learns right from the beginning that he must do something when he gets on the table, and that the only thing you will reward is the "down" behaviour.

As with all dog training, be prepared to go slower or backtrack if a dog gets stuck. Be prepared to work for a week or more on the first step if that is what is necessary.

Tunnel Training

Here are the tools you need for training the tunnel:

- Clicker

- Toy that can be thrown but does not bounce

- Food

- Wiffle ball

Use a clicker and shape the dog to go through the chute barrel.

I find that if you teach the tire first the dog gets used to the idea that he can go through a hole. Start training the tunnel using the barrel of the chute.

Use a clicker and shape the dog to go through the chute barrel. When the dog is going through, click and throw the toy. Another option is to use a wiffle-ball target in front of the chute barrel and have the dog go through the barrel to it. When the dog touches the target, click and throw the food to the dog at the wiffle ball. Try to fade the wiffle ball as soon as possible. You can do this by moving it back farther and clicking the dog before he gets to the wiffle ball. Eventually, the dog will ignore the wiffle ball, and you can remove it altogether and start to click him for coming out of the barrel. At this stage, begin to throw a toy or a food toy instead of the treats.

Once the dog will happily go through the barrel on his own (remember, no running with him) then go to the tunnel. Click the dog for being in the middle, three-quarters of the way through the tunnel, and for coming out the end. Most dogs pick up the tunnel quickly and love it. Sometimes they love it so much they will run to it if they are frustrated with something else!

Try not to click too early or your dog will turn around and come back out. I find if I accidentally do this it takes some time to straighten out the confusion but it is not the end of the world. Just go back to feeding on the other end of the tunnel.

This is where good placement of your reinforcement comes in: make sure you are throwing the toy out at the end of the tunnel for the dog. We want him driving out away from the handler to get the toy.

Contact Equipment

Training methods in the sport of agility have come so far in the last 10 years and are creating amazingly well-trained dogs at a very young age. Many people like to say this is because people are starting their dogs too early, are too eager to get into the ring, or are too competitive.

I think it is more likely that the younger dogs are benefiting from past mistakes and their handlers are using better and better techniques in the early stages of training. Without all the mistakes to undo, they are that much further ahead in the game even before they hit the ring. Because of these new, user-friendly training methods, there is really no excuse for a contact problem.

The goal in training contacts is speed and accuracy. Most of the problems people have training their dog to perform contacts happen because they try to train the speed before they have the accuracy. Remember you must train the behaviour accurately first. A dog cannot perform a dogwalk fast and proficiently if he doesn't know what he is supposed to do! You need to do your job before you can ask the dog to do his.

So just what is your job as a handler when it comes to contacts? I recommend the following steps to anyone training contacts.

- Train a distinct behaviour at the bottom of the contacts. Train a two-on two-off, a run-through, or a lie-down. Whichever you choose is up to you, but your dog needs a specific job at the bottom of the contacts and it must be something that he can repeat exactly the same way each time and something you can mark each time.

- Once you have trained that behaviour, generalize it to all locations and all types of contact equipment.

- Proof that behaviour using distractions that your dog loves (this should be over two to three months).

Susan Garrett's two-on two-off with a nose touch puts the dog's head and weight in the right spot.

- Decide before you walk into a ring what you will do if the dog makes an error.

- Track your success on each piece of equipment at your first 10 trials with the dog. Analyze your results on a regular basis and go back and clarify anything that the dog is having trouble with.

If your training stages aren't this well thought out, any confusion on the dog's part will be a result of your training.

I personally like Susan Garrett's two-on two-off method with the nose touch for training contacts. Other people train various versions of a two-on two-off without a nose touch with success, but I feel the nose touch in the initial foundation work is important to get the dog's head and weight in the right spot. It takes a bit more work but it is well worth it in the end. My last four dogs have been trained this way.

Before you start the two-on two-off training method you must find out if the dog is physically capable of getting his body in the correct position. Is there a structural problem that may inhibit the dog from performing the type of contact performance you want? It is not fair to try to train something the dog cannot physically do. Try putting the dog on a low ramp or on the bottom of a flight of stairs. Put a cookie in front of his nose and lure his head down between his front feet. Hold for about six seconds, if the dog shifts sideways or will not keep his head down he may need a bit of stretching. Do this exercise a couple of times a day and see if the dog gradually gets more comfortable. If he does not then you may have to find another method and have the dog examined for any physical problems or limitations.

I prefer the two-on two-off method with a nose touch for the following five reasons:

1. The nose-touch dog learns to go to a specific spot and put his nose between his front feet.

2. The nose touch is a repeatable behaviour to offer once he gets to the target position.

3. The nose touch requires the dog to keep his spine flat and in a straight line instead of hyper-extended. A dog that descends with his head down *must* shift his weight onto his rear end to keep himself on the board. This will lesson the impact on the dog's shoulders and neck. The sport of agility can take a toll on a dog's (or human's) body,

so if you can train a behaviour that lessens the physical stress, the dog's career in the sport will be longer.

4. If trained properly, the two-on two-off method requires the dog to shift his body weight back and drop his centre of gravity. However most people do not train this properly. The dog must touch the nose to the ground at the same time as the front feet hit the ground or else the whole nose touch is pointless.

5. With a definite stop on the end of the board, I don't have to stop running to release the dog. I can run past and get into position and I know the dog will hold his position until released. I can also turn the dog tightly off the board if necessary and can do that from anywhere. Also it keeps the dog straighter on the board as he cannot target between his feet at the end of the board *and* look back at the handler at the same time. Plus, I can use the stop on the board to catch up. Running a 36-foot dogwalk with a fast dog who has a head start is tough!

There are many aspects to contact performance. Each one should be broken down and trained separately. Let's look at the skills in small pieces. These are not in order of training; this is just a list of behaviours that need to be trained.

With each skill, count out your number of correct to incorrect responses in your training of the contacts at each stage of progression. Do not progress to the next stage until you are getting 80 to 100 per cent reliability.

Approaching
- Getting on straight

- Getting on from a 90-degree angle

- Getting on from a 180-degree approach

Running Across the Top
- Maintaining full speed across the top

- Getting off safely if there is a problem

- Striding (for running contacts)

Coming Down

- Maintaining speed down to the end

- Keeping head down on the descent

- Hitting the contact zone

- Holding for the release command (for two-on two-off)

- Placing feet on the ground immediately (for two-on two-off)

- Turning right or left off the contact on command

- Staying straight on the board

- Riding the board to the ground (for teeter)

Getting Started with Pre-Contact Work

You can start working on the foundation work for this right away with puppies and new dogs. Most of it consists of things you can do at home, and you don't need any equipment at all, just a clicker, treats, a set of stairs and a hungry dog.

Once you have done the foundation skills of hand targets, then start training plexiglass targets. I never recommend placing food on the target to get your dog to touch. Shaping will make the behaviour much stronger. Your goal is to shape the dog to touch the target with his nose, not his open mouth or paw. It needs to be a definite bop in the centre of the target.

Training the Target Behaviour

This behaviour should be started with the hand targets we addressed in Chapter 5. Once the dog will hand target, start to hold the plexiglass target.

Hold a plexiglass target in your hand and click and treat initially for looking at the target, then moving towards it, and then when the dog touches his nose on it. This progression usually happens fairly quickly as most dogs will investigate the target as soon as it is presented.

Keep your criteria in mind: your goal is to teach the dog to touch the middle of the target with his nose. Once he understands that he's supposed to touch the target, do not click the dog for scooping from the bottom or side, licking, or touching your hand or fingers. Work on this until he definitely understands he's only supposed to touch the middle of the target.

When you are shaping the target, avoid making eye contact with the dog. When you introduced the eye focus game to your dog, you taught him that if you look at him, he should look at you. I want my dog to learn to look at me only if I look at him. If I am not looking at him, I want him to look at what I am looking at. In this case, I will look at the target.

Once he is quickly and happily touching the target, start to move the behaviour to different locations. Then try it with some distractions like holding food in one hand so the dog can see it, and waiting for the dog to move away from the food to touch the target in your other hand. Once the dog can touch the target anywhere with some distractions, start to lower the target to the floor. Some dogs can go directly from the hand to the floor and others need it to be done slowly.

Gradually lower your target until your dog will offer nose touches on the target when it is placed on the floor. Watch that he isn't stepping on the target with his paw at the same time as the nose touch. If this happens, click early and throw the food slightly away from the target. As the dog turns to approach the target again, click early once more (when the dog's nose is inches in front of the target). Always throw the food behind the dog and target. Soon the dog will hang back a bit anticipating the food will be thrown behind him. Once you see him hang back, start to delay the click. Click when the dog is a bit closer to the target. Soon the dog will try to reach out with his nose but will keep his feet ready to run back and get the treat. Remember, dogs are energy efficient!

You can also shape the nose touch from the beginning by tossing the target on the floor in front of your dog and clicking and reinforcing as soon as the dog approaches the target. If your dog freezes, you can click anything the dog does to get him moving again. But make sure if he decides to lie down (or do a stationary behaviour that will not allow him to touch the target properly) that you throw your treat some place that requires the dog to get up, get the treat and approach you with the target between the two of you. This will allow you to start clicking the approach to the target again. If the dog is then hanging back too much, click on the approach and feed over top of the target to keep the dog in closer to the target.

If your dog walks toward the target, be sure to click and treat. Be patient. You may want to pick up the target one more time and toss it on the floor to get your dog's attention. If the dog lies down on the target, click and throw the food away from the target to get the dog off it. Or just pick up the target and move it so the dog has to get up. If the dog continually lies on the target pick it up and put it in your hand again for a while.

> **Contact Tip**
>
> If you are re-training contacts with an older competition dog with a bad history, you may have to pull the dog from competition until the contacts are completely re-trained.

Eventually the dog will get the idea that he should stay on his feet to touch the target.

Initially you should click even the slightest motion towards the target. As the dog begins to offer this behaviour, raise your standards and continue to shape the dog so he is actually touching the target with his nose. If he is touching the target in the centre feed right over top of the target, about three inches above the target. Make sure not to move the food hand before you click. Always click and then move your hand to feed the dog. Moving the food hand early will cause the dog to scoop or swipe the target instead of bopping it.

Move the target to different locations to encourage further learning of this behaviour. Keep the rate of reinforcement high in this early stage. If you make things too hard too soon, your dog may offer you a completely different behaviour in an attempt to figure it out. If your dog shuts down, you may have progressed too quickly — lower your criteria so that the dog can get it right and build the behaviour back up again.

Once the dog will touch the target rapidly, (about 10 touches in 15 seconds) try to remove the target and get the dog to nose touch just the floor between his front feet for one or two touches. You can do this by throwing the food after a couple nose targets to the plexiglass and then remove the plexiglass while the dog is not looking. See if the dog will come back and offer the behavior without the target plate there. Ultimately, we want the dog to learn that the target position is head down between the front feet. Try to get the dog to do the touches beside you – facing the same way as you.

I do not put a verbal cue on this behaviour. The cue to touch the target is simply the target being dropped or held out in front of them. I want the dog to understand that if he sees a target he should do everything he can to touch it. Never leave a target out that you cannot click and treat for. Keep an eye out for other peoples' targets that they forget to pick up.

Work up to 10 nose touches on the floor in 12 to 15 seconds. It will be difficult to do this if the dog or handler is making mistakes. If you can do this, you are ready to progress to the stair work.

Stair Work for Contacts

You cannot do the stair work until the dog has the following

- A solid stand and stay, with no feet moving

- A very strong nose touch to a target

- A nose touch to the ground without a target

The stairs and floor need to be two different surfaces. Dogs cannot tell the difference between yellow and blue but they can tell the difference between grass and wood.

1. Place the dog on the bottom stair in his final position and "machine gun" or rapid fire the treats. Release with your chosen release word off the stairs. Make sure you count out your rewards. Feed between front feet with the head down. Always make sure the dog leaves the stairs when released. Stand up and be still when you give your release word. You can run after the dog leaves but not before. If the dog needs help on the release, go back to plank work and work the release command there.

2. Place the dog on the bottom stair, drop the target in front of the dog, and do three to five quick nose touches. Release.

3. Drop the target and do two to three touches with the target in place. On the third click, feed the dog with his head away from the target and slide the target out. When the dog looks back he should automatically go to touch the target. Click for the nose touch to the floor. Try for two of these no-target touches and release.

4. Place the dog on the second stair and drop the target on the floor. The dog should come down the one stair to target immediately. Do three to five nose touches, treat each time, and release. Feed over the target with the dog's head low. This is when I name the behaviour. I like to wait until the dog is actually moving forward towards the target and down the stairs into position. Never use the target plate with more than two stairs. You never want the dog to run and look for a target plate.

Begin and End with Fun

Whether it is a five-minute training session or an all-day seminar, try to start out and finish up with something fun for your dog: play tug or run tunnels — do something he finds easy and fun. Always leave your training sessions with your dog thinking he is the greatest, smartest agility dog alive!

5. Repeat step 4, removing the target at some point during the touches.

6. Try to get the dog to come down to no target at all. At first the dog will be confused by this. Just wait for him to look at the floor where the target should be. Click this and feed as low to the floor as possible so that the dog has to come down for the treat with his head down. The body and head position are the most important thing at this point. The dog's spine should be in a straight line from head to tail. No looking up or arching the back. Soon the dog will anticipate that the cookie will be down there and he will try to "meet" the cookie, keeping his head looking at the floor.

7. Work towards the dog coming down one stair to target the floor with no stopping and checking back (count your errors and keep track of your success rate).

8. The dog should now start to come down two stairs to the target. Stand facing the dog or beside the dog depending on what type of stairs you are using. *Never* put food on the target plate itself.

9. Fade the target plate and try to get the nose touch to the floor between the feet, thus assuming a "target position" of two-feet-on two-off. Make sure you vary your position, as you don't want the dog to have you or your feet as part of his cue.

10. Backchain until the dog can do a full set of stairs with no stopping and checking in before he gets to the target position. (Backchaining is when you do the last behaviour first — in this case, start with one stair to target position, then two stairs, and so on.) Always feed between his front legs with his head down. Track your success. Use the target again only two to three times to help the dog if he gets stuck.

11. Proof the target position by throwing toys, running past, and so on. You are training the dog to understand the same behaviour is required no matter where you are or what else is going on.

12. Go to as many different sets of stairs as you can.

Once this is done, take the dog to the dogwalk set at two feet and redo all steps from 1 to 8 on the down ramp of the contact. Start by placing the dog in the final "position" and backchain. Do this on the A-frame at a low height as well. Teeter training is slightly different. Never let the dog do a complete piece of equipment to a target plate. He will start to look for a plate instead of learning to go to a position.

Teeter Totter

Many dogs are not given the opportunity to prepare for the teeter and wind up not liking it much at all. Dogs who really don't like the teeter or lack confidence on the teeter will jump off before it tips. Or they will perform it when the handler is right beside them but problems appear later in distance work. There are all sorts of games that can test a dog's reaction to the teeter and prepare him for it.

There are three challenging elements of teeter performance to deal with before you actually train the teeter. They are sound, height and motion.

1. Sound

An easy way to prepare for the teeter sound is to bring a young puppy into an agility class. Make sure he is really hungry! Keep him in his crate and every time someone does a teeter simply click and feed through the side of the crate. Pay attention to whether your puppy shows any reaction to the sound of the teeter. Start about 30 feet away and gradually move the puppy to within five feet of the noise, as long as he is not showing fear. If you don't have a teeter, you can use the same technique by dropping metal dog dishes or a bag of pop cans onto the floor.

2. Height

Put a small plank on a couple of stools and have the puppy walk back and forth. When he is comfortable with the low plank, put one end on the table and have him walk a plank that has only one side raised. He should walk up and down happily.

Then go to the two tables and have the dog walk a 12-foot board between two 10-inch tables. Move on to two 16-inch tables and then two 22-inch tables. Progress to the next height only if the dog is happily running across with no hesitation. Do not do the 16- or 22-inch tables with a young puppy that could fall off.

3. Motion

Use the tippy board from Chapter 7 (page 93). Let the dog walk back and forth. It is okay if the plank tips like a teeter or slides around. A wobble board (page 92) will also help accustom dogs to motion under their feet.

There are many ways to train the teeter once you're done with your pre-teeter work. The method you choose should depend on the confidence and personality of the dog and the level at which you want to compete. The easiest way to train the teeter to most dogs is with two tables.

1. Place the teeter board on two 22-inch tables. Have the dog run the plank back and forth until he is comfortable.

2. Move one table to 26 inches and have the dog tip the board down to the 22-inch table.

3. Then reverse it and have the dog tip up to the 26-inch table.

4. Then use the 22-inch table and the 16-inch table.

5. Repeat the first two steps having the dog tip down to the 16-inch table and up to the 22-inch table.

6. Then go to the 22-inch table and the 10-inch table.

7. Repeat the first two steps having the dog tip down to the 10-inch table and up to the 22-inch table.

Once the dog will do the 10- and 22-inch tables you can take out one of the tables. At each stage you need to make sure the dog is running the board completely from table to table. There should be no stopping in the middle. We do not want to even acknowledge that there is a tip point. The dog needs to learn to find the tip point and run to the other side of it as fast as possible. A dog that hesitates at the tip point lacks confidence and will likely jump off. Take your time at each stage and make sure you only progress when the dog is ready!

Testing and Proofing

Proofing is a very important part of the training program and is a step
that is often missed. This step is the one that teaches the dog that the skill
has the same requirements no matter where you are, what the weather is
like, or what is going on around you. For example, asking a dog to do a right
turn after a jump that turns him towards a wall when all the other equipment and his handler are to the left of the jump may be very hard for a dog
initially. You have to proof the command by putting the dog in as many different situations as possible.

Assessing Skills and Knowledge (ASK)

At some point in your agility-training program you are going to have to find out what you do and don't know as a team.

Both you and your dog are building skills and an agility "vocabulary" to help you communicate efficiently and quickly on course. As you have read, your training will be done in many steps. We have discussed how to break down skills and make things simple at first so the dogs are successful and enjoy the learning process. Once we have trained the skill we then need to test the dog and ourselves to see what we can do under some pressure. This is where your record keeping is vital!

ASK comes between the training and the proofing stage of the skill. It is like a "pop quiz" for you and your dog. It is the step that allows you to:

1. **Assess** what the dog has retained from the training.

2. Test your **skill** as a handler in executing the signals clearly on the first attempt.

3. Identify what **knowledge** you and your dog have and don't have as a team.

To use this to your advantage, try to be very honest in your observations, without allowing your ego to get involved. (Don't fall into the "but my dog knows this" trap!) All that you are trying to do is pinpoint any weaknesses in your training program and address them in your next training plan.

The fact that we are a team with our dogs means there are two halves that have to work simultaneously and both have to be able to execute the required skill the first time.

Here are some criteria for ASKing:

1. The exercise or skill that you wish to test should be thoroughly trained. It is not fair to test a dog on a skill barely learned. This means your training records indicate that your success rate is in the range of 80 to 90 per cent in three sessions.

2. Do not try any part of the test sequence before the actual test.

3. Use your first attempt at the sequence or skill as your final information. You and the dog should both get the sequence or skill right the first time, because you are both being tested.

This is not setting the dog up to fail. You are not going to test the dog on a skill that you are not absolutely sure that you have trained. No one is getting corrected or drilled over and over on something that they don't understand. It is simply an assessment of skills and knowledge. The result of the test will determine the next step in your training.

If you pass the test, celebrate and quit on that high note for the day. If you don't pass the test, celebrate anyway (the dog probably did what you asked and deserves a reward). Remember this is a two-way street; you both have to get it right. Make a note in your training journal that you need more work on that skill. You are a team, and for the team to reach its full potential you have to be in sync with each other at all times!

Proofing

Once you have tested your skills and feel the dog has a clear understanding and you have mastered your handling of the skill you can start to proof.

Proofing adds some stress to the dog and teaches him to work through the stressful situation. Going into a ring can be very stressful for you, and that transfers to your dog as well. Your commands may be jerky, your voice may shake or be shrill, your body may smell differently because of nerves, and your mouth may be so dry you can't get the commands out. All of this is very hard to reproduce in practice for your dog. If his whole training has consisted of his owner being calm, cool and collected at all times, what will he do when faced with an owner who is now shaking like a leaf, sweating and falling apart at the seams?

When you are proofing you may have to do things that seem silly as they are not necessarily things that will happen in a ring. So why do them? Stress is stress. If you have a flyball-crazy dog that can hold his contact position with a flyball box at the end of the contact in practice, then something as simple as a tunnel at the end of the contact in a trial should not be a problem. How about a Golden Retriever that can do a table with a person eating a hot dog sitting directly behind him? How about a Sheltie that can weave 12 poles past an open box of hot pizza? How about a Border Collie who stays on the teeter totter even with a Frisbee or tennis ball flying past him? These are all different things you can use to proof your dog. Granted, you will not likely have pizza, hotdogs, Frisbees or flyball boxes in the ring but these add a huge element of stress to the dog. If he can work through them, then a little bit of ring nerves on his owner's part will seem like a walk in the park. Think about things your dog loves and use them to proof your final behaviours. Be creative but be fair. Do not expect your dog to leave his favourite flying Frisbee if you have never taught him the "leave it" command using a Frisbee before.

Be prepared for the dog to get it wrong the first couple of times. If you throw that Frisbee and your dog breaks his trained behaviour to chase it, simply tell him, "Leave it," or have someone pick up the box of pizza, or cover the ball in the flyball box and try again. Maybe throw the Frisbee later, put the box of pizza farther away or close the lid, or use a tennis ball first and not the flyball box right away.

Be realistic in your choices and expectations. You may not be able to ever expect your JRT to stay with you if a mouse runs across the field in front of him. I could not ever expect my Border Collie, Bryn, to not chase a cat if it ran in front of her on an agility course. We do not have cats, she rarely sees them, and when she does spot one she is fascinated by them. So far no one is willing to lend me their cat so that I can train her not to chase

Think about the things your dog loves and use them to proof your final behaviours.

them! You need to be able to control whatever you use to proof the dog and in the end, let the dog have it after he does the behaviour correctly. Mice, squirrels, gofers, rabbits and cats may not be viable options.

Using one piece of agility equipment to reinforce another is not wise because you will likely never be able to prevent your dog from taking a piece of equipment on an agility course and the dog will be able to grab his own reinforcement. When you walk to that line with your dog you want to know you are the reinforcement, not the equipment. If the equipment is the reinforcement, how will you ever compete with 20 pieces of equipment in front of the dog when you are standing at the start line? The dog should perform equipment in order to get reinforced by you. Occasionally I will use the opportunity to do a piece of equipment if the dog has troubles or fears of another piece. For example, a dog that loves tunnels but is a bit worried about the teeter may be able to run to the tunnel after he has performed the teeter for me. I can count on one hand how often we have had to do this. Usually simple shaping and good placement and choice of reinforcement will be enough.

Sequencing

Sequencing is asking the dog to perform three or more obstacles in a row for one primary reinforcer. When you teach the dog to sequence, you're essentially creating a chain of behaviours.

There are different philosophies about when and how to start sequencing obstacles. Some instructors have dogs running full courses after only eight classes. Some even have their students entering their first trial after two or three sets of classes. I really believe that sequencing before the foundation and obstacle skills are fully trained, tested and proofed can lead to many of the problems we see in the ring. Asking a dog to do what he has not been thoroughly trained to do will often lead to a ring performance that includes shutting down, leaving the ring, barking, spinning, biting the handler, or generally looking disinterested in the sport.

Photograph by Photoplay's Portrait

If you ask a dog to perform a chain of behaviours when each individual link has not been taught thoroughly, the dog might look like he gets it because he's trying so hard to please you but in reality, he doesn't truly understand. You will be able to "fake it" for a while (let's face it, you can heel a dog through a Starters course and even make time!), but when the course (or chain) becomes progressively more difficult, the dog begins to get more stressed as he realizes he is not sure what you want.

As a dog stresses he will start to show avoidance signs like sniffing, barking or spinning until he sees some kind of "cue" that he recognizes and understands. Then all of a sudden it looks like he's back from the momentary brain lapse. Then things get hard again and once again the dog shuts down. The handler gets frustrated not knowing which dog is going to be in the ring with them — the one who follows happily doing what the handler asks or the one who will shut down and leave the ring. In fact it is always the same dog, but his performance varies depending on whether his understanding matches the expectations put on him in each situation. This yo-yo effect is all avoidable if your training program allows each dog to be an individual and to progress from step to step as he masters each skill, not when the human part of the team gets bored.

I understand that people love running sequences because it feels like you are doing "real agility." To keep clients happy, many instructors feel they need to allow them to do more and more, even though they know the dogs are not ready. In the long run, the dogs are the ones who pay because they're being asked to perform behaviours (or chains of behaviours) that they have not been given enough time to learn to do with confidence. A dog that looks or acts like it lacks motivation is more likely lacking confidence and understanding. Don't label a dog as de-motivated, lazy, disinterested, crazy, or out of control until you give him every opportunity to learn the skills he needs.

So what should you be sure your dog understands before you start putting multiple pieces of equipment together?

Get Out of the Picture

Often people train the equipment with their own bodies in the picture right from the beginning, usually trying to get the dogs to negotiate the equipment by running by it.

The problem with this is that the dog learns that the handler is the cue for each piece of equipment and then can't perform anything without the handler beside the equipment. This limits the potential for distance work as the dog will only allow the handler to get a certain distance before the cue becomes too vague and the dog doesn't understand it any longer.

How many times have you seen dogs start to get out in front of the handler and then actually slow their pace to reposition themselves back beside the handler? This is a dog that has a comfort zone that includes the handler somewhere beside him for each piece of equipment as that is how he first learned that piece of equipment. Once you teach something with a body in the picture, the body becomes part of the picture. You can't remove the body and still have the dog see the picture the same way.

Accuracy and Distance First

Before you start to sequence the obstacles, train accuracy and distance for each of the obstacles. If your dog can do a jump from 15 feet away, a tunnel from 20 feet away and a tire from 15 feet away, then linking a jump, tunnel and tire together will not be hard as they will already be halfway to the next obstacle when they do the first one! Contacts, weaves, jumps, tunnels and table all need to be taught independently of the handler right from the beginning.

Two at a Time

When I start to link obstacles I start with just two obstacles. Often it will be a jump to a tunnel, a tunnel to a table, a table to a jump, etc. I try hard not to have the handler run to the next obstacle but to be between the two obstacles we are linking so that the dog actually has to run past the handler to get to the next one.

A table is a great obstacle to send dogs to. A tunnel to a table provides the dogs with a nice finish point. Start with a curved tunnel and send your dog from the exit of the tunnel to the table with the arm and leg closest to the dog. Try to be in a neutral position when the dog first sees you at the exit of the tunnel and turn with the dog as he comes out. Take one step with the leg closest to the dog then indicate with the arm closest to the dog, and say, "Table!" If the dog has a good send to the table it should make perfect sense to him. Make sure there are no other pieces of equipment around other than the two you are working with. Take the one step forward to indicate that you want the dog to move forward. Lack of motion will become the cue to tell the dog to stop and come in to you. So for the sake of consistency, take one or two forward steps. Gradually add more space between the obstacles and begin to move more. Be relaxed and concentrate on facing the way you want the dog to go rather than running or being frantic. The dog should be working ahead of the handler, not holding back beside the handler or behind the handler. We want the dog to learn it is acceptable to drive ahead to the next obstacle when your body language tells him to go forward.

Work on getting the behaviour accurately, then work for more speed and enthusiasm, then add in the distraction of maybe a jump sitting off to the side someplace, and then go to another location.

Using Targets

Use a target or lure to help the dog understand what you want. Personally I think every obstacle is actually a target and can help draw or lure the dog to the next obstacle if each one is trained and reinforced properly. But

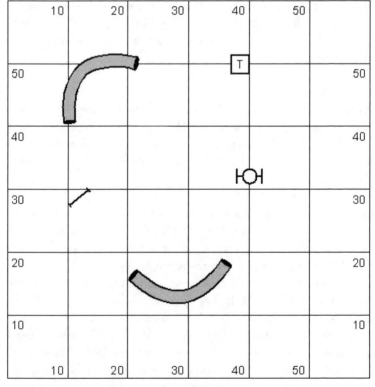

When your dog is successful with two obstacles, link up more at 90-degree angles.

The Three–S Rule

Three-S means "Simplify, get Success, then Step it up a notch." If, for example, you set up a sequence and for whatever reason, you and your dog just can't get through it properly in two attempts, then it is time to simplify. Make sure the dog understands the basics of the skill. Have you trained the basic skills to fluency? Once the dog gets consistent success at the simplified sequence, then you are ready to step it up a notch by gradually making the sequence a little harder.

---

sometimes the use of a toy or wiffle ball target can help the dog drive out in front of the handler more confidently.

Some rules for using the toy or any target that isn't an obstacle would be to only use it three times and then wait for the dog to offer an attempt at the behaviour without the target there. For example, if you have a dog that needs some help going ahead and taking a jump after a tunnel without the handler moving much, you could throw or place a toy on the ground on the other side of the jump as the dog is coming out of the tunnel. This will help him focus on the jump and the toy and not the handler.

If the dog can drive ahead to the jump three times in a row with the toy there, it is time to get rid of the toy and see if the dog will attempt to go to the jump on his own. Notice I did not say that the dog had to actually do the jump, but he needs to make an effort towards the jump. So if the dog comes out of the tunnel and runs towards the jump I would click and throw the toy past the jump. The dog is "marked" for moving forward towards the jump and the placement of the reward encourages him to finish the jump. After a few repetitions of this, the dog will anticipate that the toy will be coming. He will race out over the jump on his own, at which time you can click for going over the jump and celebrate by throwing him the toy and having a great game of tug! Using a toy as a target this way can greatly speed up your training if you do it correctly.

So what about a dog that runs around the jump to get the toy? First, back chain the dog to do the jump to the toy. Set him up to be successful by making it harder, but not impossible, to go around the jump. Wings on the jump or baby gates can help him get it right. Once he goes over the jump to the toy successfully three times in row, then add in the tunnel to the jump to the toy.

You can also have someone stand near the toy and remove it if the dog runs around the jump. The only problem with this is that we are actually adding in another target to fade… the person! This is not insurmountable but it is a factor if you are going to use another person for this purpose. I prefer to rely on my "leave it" command and try to make it easier for the dog to get it right. However there are always exceptions to any rule. If the dog is not super toy motivated, calling him off a toy may make it worse. In this case, you might just let the dog grab the toy and celebrate with him for grabbing a toy! Then go back and make it harder for him to run around the jump.

Adding Obstacles

When my dog is consistently successful with two obstacles and I'm ready to link up three or four obstacles, I start with 90-degree angles. I want to make it easy for the dog to see the obstacles in front of him and still have the physical support of the handler without having the handler at a full-out run. The handler will need to work on facing where he wants the dog to go, using the correct arm and leg to direct the dog and not running right up to any piece of equipment. A handler running frantically beside a dog is a very big distraction. I don't want to be putting distractions into the sequencing until the sequence is learned accurately and then with speed. I want the dog to drive out to the next obstacle on his own. After all, we want the dog running ahead of us on course, not behind us!

A small amount of movement is acceptable but I really want to try to get the dog to move ahead and take what is in front of him as quickly as possible. As long as his handler is facing the direction of a piece of equipment then the dog should go to it. I really like my dogs to start out being more obstacle than handler focused. I can add the distraction of me running with the dog after he is confidently going out ahead of me to the equipment I am facing. Let's face it, I am never going to be faster than my dogs so they need to learn – right from the beginning – that I am not going to be ahead of them all the time.

In the end, we want a dog that will look ahead for the next piece of equipment and is comfortable running in front of the handler and performing equipment on his own. I can add in my cue system for my crosses and other handling maneuvers once the dog is confidently working ahead of me. It is very difficult to teach a dog to do front and rear crosses if he will not go ahead to jumps.

If you work on your individual obstacle and sequencing skills carefully and allow your dog to be completely comfortable with those skills first, the next step in the behaviour chain will be that much easier!

Handling your Dog

If you follow the training advice in this book and your dog learns his foundation work and becomes proficient at performing obstacles independently and on cue, your next step is to learn how to handle your dog.

Handling is using body language to move the dog through the course. Handling work should start with some of the one-obstacle exercises like the front cross, the rear cross and the wrap. Then, when dogs can run a sequence of several obstacles, looking ahead to commit to the next piece of equipment, we can start to add our body language.

When I teach handling, I use no verbal commands except "okay" as a release to move, "go" to go ahead of me, and verbal praise when the dog gets it right.

Your goal is to develop a handling language with your dog using your arms, legs, feet, hips and shoulders without using your voice. The reason we are not using our voice when teaching and practicing handling is that we want to see how our body motions and cues affect the dog. We can't ask him what makes sense to him, so we have to experiment. Once you begin to handle short sequences silently, you may see ways that you need to change or modify your handling to get the dog to understand you.

Handling is a vast subject that is another book unto itself. My advice is to find a good instructor with a consistent system of cues that his or her dog understands and executes successfully.

Taking Classes

One of the first things people say to me when they get hooked on this sport is, "My spouse/friend/dad is going to build me a set of equipment." I try not to cringe when I hear this. I think the pitfalls of training in isolation are far greater than the advantages. In my opinion, getting to a class once or twice a week is the best way to stay current and be successful.

Here are 10 reasons to sign up for classes instead of trying to run courses on your own:

1. Solid Foundations

An experienced instructor has a thorough training program and will help you progress at a speed that is suitable for you and your dog. He should also be able to help you develop a consistent system of cues that works for you and your dog. Otherwise, you may end up with a system of "default handling" — flinging yourself around to get the dog to do what you want.

Many dogs do well in Starters classes and by the time they get to Masters, completely shut down. This comes from training skills that are too hard for the dog too early and inconsistent handling. The dogs become confused, the handlers get frustrated, and the rewards diminish for both. Pretty soon, no one is having fun any more.

2. Raising the Bar

Being in classes forces you to try new techniques. I find people who train in isolation are less able to try new ideas and accept constructive criticism. They're often less willing to try techniques that they can't do well the first time they try. In my experience, as you get better at agility and things get harder, you never do things well right off the bat! There are too many variables. Just because you have trouble mastering a skill doesn't mean you should give up on it. But when you're working alone, it's too easy to focus on the skills that come easily and that you find fun instead of the skills you don't do well.

3. Doggie Distractions

Class also helps your dog meet and get used to different dogs. Your dog won't be able to focus on the course at a trial if he's preoccupied with the canine spectators at ringside. A class will help your dog get used to working around doggy buddies. While you often see the same dogs week to week, someone always seems to miss a class here and there. When a dog that has been away appears again, it's distracting to the dogs for a bit. This is a great training opportunity. Use it!

4. A Place to Proof

The class environment helps dogs generalize. There is nothing wrong with practicing at home. But we all know that what happens in the back yard does not always carry through to the ring. The dog has to transfer all his skills to new locations before you trial. Can you do that serpentine in class as well as you did it in your back yard? Does the dog hit his pole entries or contacts as well in class as at home? A regular class tests the skills that are easy on your home turf.

5. Friendly Feedback

Classes help you figure out what went wrong. Instructors and fellow students help us in the search for the perfect handler inside us all. It's amazing how much you can learn by watching other people work their dogs, and being able to have others help you work through your handling problems.

Everyone needs someone there to say "you moved too fast" or "you called her while she was over that bar" or "you were looking right at that tunnel!" Unless you plan to haul out the video camera and actually tape all your practices, sit down and analyze the video, and go back and try to rework it, you will never really know what you're doing to cause the dog to make mistakes.

6. Soundness Advice

Other people may pick up on signs of lameness or injury that the handler can't see. When you're running the dog, it's often hard to tell when the dog looks sore or which leg he's limping on. Someone who watches your dog move on a regular basis can pick up a change in gait, movement or even behaviour very quickly. This is invaluable.

7. Rest Stops

In a class, you're forced to rest your dog. When you are all alone there is no one there waiting to go next. You can work your dog for 20 minutes straight and never even know it! It is important to work in short sessions of two to three minutes and rest dogs often. Taking turns with other people forces you to work quickly and efficiently and focus on quality, not quantity.

8. Ring Crew

Assistants or other class members can help with setting and re-setting equipment, holding dogs, throwing and removing toys, timing your sequences, and many other vital tasks. Plus, certain training techniques can be difficult to do all alone.

9. Variety of Course

A regular class allows you to have a different set-up each week. Moving a field of equipment alone can be a daunting task, so many people leave their equipment in the same spot for long periods of time. When they say "weave" the dog has learned to go to the area where the equipment is. The dog is not necessarily linking the name with the piece of equipment, or watching you to direct him to the right obstacle. Moving things around ensures thorough learning and keeps things fun and interesting.

10. Support Systems

My very favourite reason for class is the support system from other class members. We all have bad days or bad trials sometimes but there is always someone there to keep things in perspective, keep you from taking out your frustration on the dog, or run your dog through a sequence to convince you that the problem really is your handling, and your dog is capable of running it.

Choosing an Instructor

Just as important as taking a class is having a good instructor. A good instructor is someone who:

- Competes with his own dogs on a regular basis. Trialing and watching other handlers run is the way to stay on the cutting edge of the sport. Training methods are changing so fast that instructors have to be actively involved to stay on top of things.

- Continually educates herself. Ask your potential instructor which high-quality, skill-building seminars she's attended lately.

- Is versatile, creative and open-minded. He shouldn't have a "my way or the highway" attitude and should be able to relate to a variety of dogs and handlers.

- Works the size and speed of dog you work with. These factors affect handling techniques.

- Understands many breed-related issues. Just because an instructor can motivate and bring the out best in her own dogs doesn't mean she'll be able to understand yours.

- Uses positive training techniques. Good trainers never bully dogs into doing the sport.

- You admire. Pick an instructor whose manner of relating to his dogs is appealing and whose handling style you'd like to emulate.

- Is a skilled teacher and communicator. He should be able to break skills down into learnable segments so you can easily understand and teach your own dog.

- Will not push you to enter fun matches or trials before you are truly ready. The problems caused by inexperienced or stressed dogs running away, showing aggression or taking equipment unsafely can, at the least, set you and your dog back or at at worst, cause tragic injury.

So next time registration for classes rolls around, sign up! You won't regret it. If you can't find a good instructor in your area, get a training group together and organize regular training sessions.

Even people who live in isolated parts of the country can usually find a training group and an instructor within driving distance to train regularly with. It is so important to have someone there to help you with the multitude of things that go wrong — and celebrate when things go right!

FOUNDATION SKILLS

Week One

OBEDIENCE									
Eye Focus									
Walk Stop and Look									
Sit									
Down									
Give it/Get it									
Backup									
Hand Target									
Say Hello									
Recall									

Week One

FOUNDATION WORK										
Rear End Work	Stool work									
	Ladder									
	Jump bumps									
Targets	Hand									
	Wiffle Ball									
	Plexi Glass									
Directionals	Right									
	Left									
	Out									
	Away									
	Look Back									
	Turn									
	Moving Wait									

	Week Two							Week Three							Week Four						

	Week Two							Week Three							Week Four						

FOUNDATION SKILLS

			Week One							
FLATWORK	Side/Close									
	Swing									
	Around									
	Front									
	Go									
	Footwork Front Cross									
	Rear Cross									
	Wrap/Post Turn									

			Week One							
PRE-OBSTACLE TRAINING	Wobble Board									
	Tippy Board									
	Jump Standards									
	Jump Bumps									
	Table									
	Plank Work Flat on ground									
	Elevated									
	Weaves 2 Poles									
	3 Poles									
	Chute Poles									

	Week Two	Week Three	Week Four

	Week Two	Week Three	Week Four

FOUNDATION SKILLS

			Week One								
ONE OBSTACLE TRAINING	Jump	Grid Work									
		One Jump Work									
		Directionals									
		Distance									
		Table									
		Tunnel									
		Tire									
	Contacts	Hand Touch									
		Nose Touch on Plexi									
	Stair Work	Release Word									
		Stay In Position									
	Teeter Work	2 Tables									
	Sequencing	Jump									
		Tunnel									
		Table									
		Tire									

	Week Two	Week Three	Week Four

Recommended Reading Material

Title	Author
Culture Clash	Jean Donaldson
Dog Sport Magazine	www.dogsportmagazine.com
Clean Run Magazine	www.cleanrun.com
Ruff Love	Susan Garrett
Shaping Success	Susan Garrett
Purely Positive Training	Sheila Booth
Ex-celerated Learning	Pam Reid
Power of Positive Dog Training	Pat Miller
The Third Way	Chris Bach
Click for Joy	Melissa Alexander
How Dogs Learn	Burch/Bailey
Animals in Translation	Temple Grandin

Agility Associations

Agility Association of Canada	www.aac.ca
United States Dog Agility Association	www.usdaa.com
North American Dog Agility Council	www.nadac.com
American Kennel Club	www.akc.org
Canadian Kennel Club	www.ckc.ca
Canine Performance Events	www.k9cpe.com

Index

N

O

P

R

Really Reliable Recall. Train Your Dog to Come When Called, DVD. Leslie Nelson
Right on Target. Taking Dog Training to a New Level. Mandy Book & Cheryl Smith
Stress in Dogs. Martina Scholz & Clarissa von Reinhardt
Tales of Two Species. Essays on Loving and Living With Dogs. Patricia McConnell
The Dog Trainer's Resource. The APDT Chronicle of the Dog Collection. Mychelle
Blake (*ed*)
The Dog Trainer's Resource 2. The APDT Chronicle of the Dog Collection. Mychelle
Blake (*ed*)
The Thinking Dog. Crossover to Clicker Training. Gail Fisher
Therapy Dogs. Training Your Dog To Reach Others. Kathy Diamond Davis
Training Dogs. A Manual (reprint). Konrad Most
Training the Disaster Search Dog. Shirley Hammond
Try Tracking. The Puppy Tracking Primer. Carolyn Krause
Visiting the Dog Park, Having Fun, and Staying Safe. Cheryl S. Smith
When Pigs Fly. Train Your Impossible Dog. Jane Killion
Winning Team. A Guidebook for Junior Showmanship. Gail Haynes
Working Dogs (reprint). Elliot Humphrey & Lucien Warner

HEALTH & ANATOMY, SHOWING
An Eye for a Dog. Illustrated Guide to Judging Purebred Dogs. Robert Cole
Annie On Dogs! Ann Rogers Clark
Another Piece of the Puzzle. Pat Hastings
Canine Cineradiography DVD. Rachel Page Elliott
Canine Massage. A Complete Reference Manual. Jean-Pierre Hourdebaigt
Canine Terminology (reprint). Harold Spira
Breeders Professional Secrets. Ethical Breeding Practices. Sylvia Smart
Dog In Action (reprint). Macdowell Lyon
Dog Show Judging. The Good, the Bad, and the Ugly. Chris Walkowicz
Dogsteps DVD. Rachel Page Elliott
The Healthy Way to Stretch Your Dog. A Physical Theraphy Approach. Sasha Foster
and Ashley Foster
The History and Management of the Mastiff. Elizabeth Baxter & Pat Hoffman
Performance Dog Nutrition. Optimize Performance With Nutrition. Jocelynn Jacobs
Positive Training for Show Dogs. Building a Relationship for Success Vicki Ronchette
Puppy Intensive Care. A Breeder's Guide To Care Of Newborn Puppies. Myra Savant
Harris
Raw Dog Food. Make It Easy for You and Your Dog. Carina MacDonald
Raw Meaty Bones. Tom Lonsdale
Shock to the System. The Facts About Animal Vaccination... Catherine O'Driscoll
Tricks of the Trade. From Best of Intentions to Best in Show, Rev. Ed. Pat Hastings
Work Wonders. Feed Your Dog Raw Meaty Bones. Tom Lonsdale
Whelping Healthy Puppies, DVD. Sylvia Smart

Dogwise.com your source for quality books, ebooks, DVDs, training tools and treats.

We've been selling to the dog fancier for more than 25 years and we carefully screen our products for quality information, safety, durability and FUN! You'll find something for every level of dog enthusiast on our website www.dogwise.com or drop by our store in Wenatchee, Washington.